71% of employees are not
engaged at work.

19% of employees are actively
disengaged at work.

Only 10% of employees
are engaged at work.

IT'S TIME TO JOIN THAT 10%

*In Western Europe (according to The State of the
Global Workplace 2021 report by Gallup)

THIS BOOK IS FOR...

I wrote this book for people who feel just like I did 10 years ago – stuck. Don't get me wrong, I wasn't totally miserable at work. In fact, I was good at it, too good you could say, as I ended up promoted into roles I didn't really want (and, if I'm honest, didn't suit me anyway). The truth is, I was not fulfilled, excited or at all energised about what I spent 40+ hours a week doing.

So, this book is for you if:

- The daily grind is zapping your energy.

- Your work is not fulfilling or making you happy (no matter how good at it you are).

- You are currently feeling stuck in your job or perhaps uncertainty is creeping in about whether it really is the thing you want to spend the rest of your working life doing.

- In an ideal world, you'd be doing something different but for one reason or another you've found yourself here and are now wondering if it's even possible to change.

- You'd like to explore an alternative in a structured way with me coaching you every step of the way.

- You long for change but fear of the unknown, or a salary change is holding you back.

I would also like to say that getting unstuck is all about working out what is right for you, and that's not necessarily a dramatic leap from where you are. In fact, I help a lot of people find more suitable roles that make them a lot happier within the same industry, or even the same company. But it *could* be a big change. At this stage, we don't know, so join me and let's find out...

THIS BOOK WILL...

- Guide you through a process and create a much-needed space for you to really reflect on what's important to you – your vision, values and so much more.

- Help you work out where you would ideally like to be and give you a roadmap for getting there.

- Gently coach you through the journey with thought-provoking questions that will have you looking at your life in a new way.

Often, we don't take a moment out to check if we're on the right track, we just keep our head down and work hard. The thing is, it's so easy to get pushed down a certain path, which can start with family and end with managers, and one day waking up wondering how on earth you got here and whether it's even possible to do anything about it. At that point, any kind of change can seem overwhelming, and in my experience, people tend to talk themselves out of taking action.

And I'm all about action.

After going through this process:

- You will have learned something important about yourself.

- You will have a clear vision of success and will be making progress towards achieving your goal.

- You and those around you will have a better understanding of what your values are and find making the right decision for you easier.

- You will feel a lot happier, more confident and have increased self-belief (you won't be getting in your own way anymore).

- You will be well on your way to living the kind of life where you get out of bed on a Monday morning with a smile on your face, looking forward to the day ahead. You'll be *showing up* instead of turning up in work.

- As you build a new sense of purpose, your colleagues and family will notice this shift in mentality and behaviour; they will see happiness radiating through your life.

The work we'll do is deep. You need to be honest with yourself, reconnecting with desires and ideas you may have buried away for many years, but if you put the effort in, then you'll start moving from stuck to empowered.

TESTIMONIALS

"Jeff's book provides a practical guide for people who want to take more control of shaping their futures… Jeff has many years' experience as an educator, facilitator and trusted advisor. The depth of his knowledge is transmitted in the human stories and practical strategies he brings to life."

MIKE PEGG, FOUNDER OF THE POSITIVE ENCOURAGER AND MANAGING DIRECTOR OF THE STRENGTHS ORGANISATION LTD.

Mike has been helping people, teams and organisations to build on their strengths and achieve their pictures of success for more than fifty years.

———

"Jeff has had a profound impact on the culture of our business, and in particular – our leadership team. He takes time to listen to people, to really understand their personal values – while at the same time challenges them ferociously to be the best person they can be."

PHIL MCNULTY, SALES DIRECTOR AT ADD PEOPLE.

Phil is responsible for operations and a sales team of 70 people at a digital marketing company.

———

"Books are made for certain times... and Jeff's book is made for now.

Giving you tools and a narrative to navigate you through your thoughts and create clarity, this book will either be devoured quickly and set you on a track, or gently provoke you to consider your decisions. That's a rare gift to be able to work in that paradox."

KIRSTY MAC, BUSINESS SORTER-OUTERER AND EXECUTIVE COACH WHO HAS GUIDED PEOPLE THROUGH CHANGE FOR MANY YEARS.

MEET JEFF WEIGH

Jeff Weigh is:

- On a mission to help as many people as possible get unstuck and create fulfilling careers.

- A leadership coach and co-founder of Ignite Performance Coaching, a company providing learning and development for leaders and individuals within organisations.

- Co-Founder of UKRunChat community, which today is one of the largest online running communities with over 75,000 followers on Twitter.

- A podcaster on work-life balance, for which he has interviewed entrepreneurs, thought leaders and sportspeople, including: Kriss Akabusi, Greg Searle, Mike Pegg, Kirsty Mac, Chris Barez-Brown, Professor Damian Hughes, Cody Royle and Kate Richardson-Walsh.

- A dad to three children, aged 6-16, who he draws inspiration from each day.

He has:

- Been stuck in a job that made him miserable.

- Taken a job he hated due to financial pressures (he lasted three months).

- Got his career unstuck and vowed to help as many people as possible go from stuck to fulfilled in their careers.

- Developed a powerful live one-day digital workshop that can take anyone from stuck and fed up with their job to energised and excited about their career.

- The wisdom of 17 years' experience inspiring businesses, teams and managers to act boldly and be more courageous.

- Been asked to speak at numerous learning and development events across the world, empowering and enabling over 100 organisations and 10,000 employees over the last 17 years.

- Numerous professional qualifications, including: an Institute of Leadership & Management level 7 qualification in coaching and mentoring and an NLP & Hypnotherapy Master Practitioner qualification.

- Co-hosted a local radio show called Kickstart which focused on how people could motivate themselves at the start of each week.

- Spent a week running around the UK (2014), running 5 x 10kms each day, with his friend Joe Williams and the UKRunChat community.

- Run the London (2010) and Manchester (2013) marathons, raising money for CLIC Sargent and The Christie Charitable Fund.

Find out more about what Jeff is up to via his website or social media channels:

🏠 **WWW.STUCKNOWWHAT.COM**

in **WWW.LINKEDIN.COM/IN/JEFFWEIGH/**

🐦 **TWITTER.COM/JEFF_WEIGH**

📷 **WWW.INSTAGRAM.COM/JEFFWEIGH/**

OR

Search for 'Jeff Weigh' on Spotify or Apple Podcasts

to treat your ears to his awesome podcast where he regularly shares little nuggets of insight, inspiration and interviews with interesting individuals from the world of sport, business and academia.

www.get-known.co.uk

I dedicate this book to anyone who finds themselves stuck at points in their life.

Maintain hope and keep going.

Like me, your guide(s) will appear when you need them.

ST CK!

U

NOW WHAT?

How to reignite your
career when it feels flat

Jeff Weigh

CONTENTS

—❝—

*Choose a job you love
and you'll never have to work a
day in your life.*

CONFUCIUS

—❞—

HOW TO USE
THIS BOOK

Becoming unstuck is easy in many ways and a little more complex in others. Throughout this book I will nudge and challenge you as much as I will encourage and celebrate you.

I've sprinkled some *questions to consider* throughout which are designed to be a time to pause and reflect on certain sections of the book and ask yourself how it relates to your life.

To help you get the most out of this book I have put together a supporting workbook to help you consolidate all of your thoughts around becoming unstuck and act as a tool for you to reference and review your progress. It is full of trackers, worksheets and resources that you'll need to be able to complete the exercises in the book.

There is also space to brainstorm ideas and any inspiration that comes to light from my *questions to consider*.

STUCKNOWWHAT.COM/RESOURCES

WHAT IS THE PROBLEM AND WHY ARE SO MANY OF US STUCK?

'The important thing about a problem is not the solution, but the strength we gain in finding a solution.'

SENECA THE YOUNGER

Your alarm is set for 6:30am. This gives you enough time to hit the snooze button, up to four times on average[1] and check your social media before thinking about work and making your way to the shower.

Can't you see, the problem has already begun?!

You've already lost 36 minutes of your day, but perhaps you don't realise this because you're caught up in your routine. However, in reality, your routine isn't serving you well. In fact, it's become a bit of a grind.

Showered and dressed, you can't resist checking your social media once more before heading off on your commute.

Breakfast on the go. This has been the case for some time. You tell yourself that your first coffee or tea or energy drink will kickstart you into action once you get into the office.

On your commute, an average of 59 minutes in the UK[2], you allow yourself to be distracted by any number of things, including listening to music, reading the news, playing games, checking your social media, messaging friends and getting a heads-up by checking your work emails.

Before you know it, you're there. Back at your workplace. The one you left 14 hours ago. Stepping through the door, you're already telling yourself: let's do this, or here we go again – another day, another dollar! For some of you this has evolved into: same shit, different day!

Once your drink has been made and some transactional conversations have been enjoyed with Barbara in Accounts and Dave in IT, it's time to face the daily grind and do some WORK. Whilst this is work, it isn't really working.

Today, like any other day, begins with you opening up your emails and checking what's come in overnight or first thing. This process can take you anywhere between 10–15 min-

This is work,

yet this isn't working.

utes, if you're disciplined. If you're not and you allow your-self to go off down a rabbit hole checking random emails or allowing yourself to be distracted by team members arriving at work, it can take between 30–45 minutes.

That's the first hour gone, time for a refill.

It's 9:30am and you're bracing yourself for the first in a series of back-to-back meetings that will take you up to lunch. Short on time to brief your team, or your co-work-ers, you deliver a couple of key messages and hope that this sets them up for the day. Dan, the designated number two in the team, will have to pick up the rest. With little or no opportunity to refuel or pee, you ponder where your next caffeine fix will come from.

Meeting follows meeting follows meeting and, before you know it, you're back at your desk trying to catch up and understand what you've missed. Only you don't ever really catch up. You just take work home instead. And you don't really get the time to understand what you missed because that's gone and been dealt with already. You can already see how the afternoon goes because you have that clear picture in your head.

Why?

The problem is that you feel stuck. This is work, yet this isn't working.

This is the grind that many employees and managers face each day.

It doesn't end when you log off from work and head home either.

Whatever your responsibilities and circumstances are at home, the likelihood is that you're spending part of your evening responding to emails or completing work tasks.

Perhaps you even tell yourself that by catching up at home you're getting ahead for the following day!

Before you read any further, here's a quick test to see if you're caught up in the daily grind:

1. Do you take work home?

2. Do you answer emails in the evening and/or weekends?

3. Are you still awake at midnight watching just one more episode on Netflix (or similar)?

4. Are you waking in the night?

5. Do you have a gym membership but rarely go?

6. Do you get home and have no energy to exercise?

7. Is your diet/lifestyle suffering because of your work?

8. Are you drinking more alcohol?

9. Do you set an alarm for the morning?

10. Do you hit the snooze button (more than once)?

If you've answered YES to five or more of the questions above, something clearly isn't working. You're probably reading this book because you can identify with some of the issues above, even if (on the outside) it appears that you're leading a successful career.

Why are you feeling:

- Unfulfilled at work?

- Dissatisfied with where you are in life?

- Like you can no longer motivate your team?

- Unhappy, and finding it affecting your mental health?

The short answer is: this is work, yet this isn't working.

You're not alone.

Others are starting to feel isolated at work, which is compounding the problem.

A recent study[3] found 40% of employees are feeling isolated at work. This sense of isolation can lead to disengagement or cause employees to go so far as to find new jobs.

Let's pause for a moment to reflect on this. Imagine that, out of every 10 colleagues you're currently working alongside, four of them are feeling isolated right now. I wonder if you know who they are.

From the *Guardian*[4]: 'There's no one at the place where I spend much of my waking life to whom I can turn when I want to confide my fears, to moan about the upper echelons, to worry about what's happening at home.'

This is becoming more and more common in the workplace, even for those people who are perceived to be enjoying a successful career. Like you, these people have found that work has become unfulfilling and more a means to an end.

Confirmation

Take the case of someone I know, who spent the majority of his 40-year career working for the same company. He worked long hours and took overtime whenever it was offered. When I asked if he enjoyed his work, the short answer was 'no'.

You see, a combination of management and internal processes made his life more stressful and dissatisfying. The time in the year for annual appraisals and performance reviews only added to this stress and caused him more unhappiness.

When the opportunity to take early retirement was presented to him, he jumped at the chance. However, years after retiring he would still wake up in the middle of the night worrying about whether or not he'd completed the job correctly or filed everything away!

On reflection, it's easy to see now that his important personal values weren't aligned with the way the organisation was operating. It is not uncommon to see organisational values conflicting with personal values and you'll discover more about this as you read further into the book.

He worked at a time when the majority of people took a job after leaving school that became a job or career for life. He worked to provide for his family, so enjoying his job was seen as less important. However, he did have his own opinions and wouldn't shy away from putting them forward.

Now this may seem like an extreme scenario to share, but it's not. If you're not careful, life does creep up on you. In fact, it may be doing so already.

Without realising it or paying much attention, you may have found yourself in a role that you're not happy with. It doesn't bring you joy each day, but you're torn because it pays the bills.

However, there is still hope.

If you could just find that passion again. The passion you had when you took the job in the first place. Or the passion you had when you arrived at this company. Or the passion that you have when you consider your dream job! If you could just go back to doing the work that better matched your skills...

Telling yourself that you were happier then and enjoying your work more, isn't really going to help you now. You've moved on since then and, more to the point, you may not even know which roles actually match your skills.

If there was a way to somehow match the work you do with some of your values – your values being the reasons that you get out of bed in the first place.

You may be looking:

- for answers
- at options
- for something different

Worse than that, you may be scared of:

- change
- stepping into the unknown
- admitting that you're in the wrong job

Fast forward to the end of your life. It's difficult not to imagine how you might reflect on your years when you read the book (or blog post) by Bronnie Ware, *The Top Five Regrets of the Dying*.

1. I wish I'd had the courage to live a life true to myself, not the life others expected of me.

2. I wish I hadn't worked so hard.

3. I wish I'd had the courage to express my feelings.

4. I wish I had stayed in touch with my friends.

5. I wish that I had let myself be happier.

Hope

There is hope, and that's what I'm going to provide you with throughout this book. A lot of people are experiencing some or all of what I've described already, and I've helped them, or I am continuing to help them.

This book is the culmination of what I've learned from being able to help other people. In fact, I too have found myself in these types of scenarios on different occasions in my life.

I was working for M&S Money back in 2009 when I met (for the first time) the blind adventurer Miles Hilton-Barber. He opened my mind (and eyes) to the possibility of making changes in my life.

Before I met him, we'd exchanged just a couple of telephone calls. I should have realised that my life was going to take a turn when he left me a voicemail saying, 'Hi Jeff, buddy, great to hear from you and sorry I missed your call. I'd love to talk some more and find out what you have in mind.'

I'd never met him, yet Miles had such a profound effect on me and my thinking. I went home that night and replayed the voicemail to my wife. He was so personal and yet so authentic.

This is a guy who until his early 20s had sight. But on applying to go into the South African Airforce, it was discovered that he (and his brother Geoff) had a genetic hereditary eye disease that meant he would go blind. Miles lived within the limitations of his blindness until his brother (who had gone blind as well) decided to set sail from Durban in South Africa to the west coast of Australia on his own using speech output technology. He became the first blind person to cross an ocean solo. This inspired Miles to consider his own limitations.

Alongside the many inspiring stories and achievements that Miles shared the day that he came into M&S Money, I kept playing over and over in my mind the following quote: 'The only limits in life are those we accept ourselves.'

This was my catalyst and would later become the quote on the back of my first business card!

— Questions to consider —

We've reached our first little challenge. It's time to grab your workbook (you can get it here if you haven't already stucknowwhat.com/resources), take a moment to really think about these questions and write down your honest answers in your workbook.

1. (Right now) Is work really working for you?

2. Are you ready to consider a life of less grind?

3. Instead of feeling isolated at work, who could you turn to?

4. Of the 'Top Five Regrets of the Dying', which ones stir you the most and get that fire flaming inside you?

5. What if you could change? What would you do instead?

THE TRUE COST OF STAYING STUCK

*'If you don't prioritise your life,
someone else will.'*

GREG MCKEOWN – AUTHOR OF *ESSENTIALISM*

Now imagine for a moment that you've allowed yourself to entertain thoughts about your own vision of success and what's important to you (your values). What difference do you see?

Cast your mind back to the 6am alarm going off… You can see how a typical day plays out. Now consider doing that every day for a year, or two. Or the last five years!

Wow, that's exhausting. It's exhausting (for you) and it's worrying (for your employer), but it's more than that too.

Who wants to be doing the same thing over and over again? The short answer is: no one. You're not designed that way, and neither am I. You've been designed to evolve and grow.

Einstein said, 'insanity is *doing the same thing over and over again and expecting a different outcome.*'

He knew a thing or two.

Take a look around you in the office and notice how many of your colleagues or peers are doing just that: what they've always done. Are they part of the 40% who are feeling isolated at work? (Survey shared in Chapter 1.)

Now pause for a moment and look at yourself over the last two to three years and answer honestly: do you feel like this too?!

It's OK if this *has* been you and, likewise, it's OK if this *still* is you. How you wish to continue living your life right now is up to you.

Are you stuck in a rut?

I don't know you or your circumstances right now. Therefore, it would be wrong of me to jump to conclusions and suggest you need to break out of this cycle and this place that you have got yourself into.

What I do know, and what I have seen (repeatedly) throughout my career, firstly as an employee, and then as a self-employed consultant and coach, is this:

- People get stuck in a rut.

- They get stuck for a whole host of reasons and don't know how to get out.

- They try this and that, but it doesn't work. Inevitably it doesn't work because they are trying to get out of their rut using the thinking that got them in there in the first place.

At first you don't even notice that you're in a rut.

It's worth just reminding yourself what an actual rut is. A rut is: a habit or pattern of behaviour that has become dull and unproductive but is hard to change.

It doesn't have to be a rut; it could easily be any one of the following:

- Being stuck in a boring routine.

- Being caught up with the daily grind.

- A feeling of being on a treadmill.

Being in a rut is only the start of your potential problems.

The manager who was in a Diet Coke rut

Back in 2016 I was facilitating leadership programmes for a large, well-known builders' merchant in the UK. In one particular group there was one female manager, which is rare as the industry is well known for having predominantly male employees. What struck me about her quite early on was that she was comfortable to challenge and happy to share.

What also struck me was her ability to drink a lot of Diet Coke each day (and mainly in the morning)! When I enquired about her insatiable desire for Diet Coke, she divulged that it was her way of getting through each morning. She was also dieting at this stage and this reaffirmed in her own mind that drinking Diet Coke was OK.

Curious to find out more about her diet and how she was getting on, I probed a little further and asked more questions:

- What's your goal (vision of success)?

- Have you been that weight before?

- Do you have a picture from when you were that weight?

- What type of diet were you doing?

- How would you feel when you hit your goal (vision of success)?

- What's working and not working so far?

I avoided asking her the 'magic number' that people generally aim for when looking to lose weight as this is often personal and people don't want to share. However, it was important to get the goal from her (which she did later share).

You'd be right to ask at this stage, how is a story about Diet Coke and weight loss linked to someone being in a rut? The manager was very forthcoming with sharing her answers and a short open conversation quickly got us to the crux of the problem. The diet itself (and the Diet Coke) had come about because this manager had got herself into a rut at work.

She wasn't happy at work. When she started in the building business, she didn't know what she wanted to do in her career. She'd previously worked for her dad in the building game. She had progressed well and had been offered the chance to further develop herself as a leader. She grabbed the opportunity to be a branch manager with both hands, as people often do when someone else is offering them a (potential) way out of their current rut.

It soon became apparent that she was struggling with motivation to complete the coursework, which was primarily branch and results focused. Whilst her branch was performing OK, she'd already started having thoughts of 'what if?'

'What if?' thoughts might include:

- What if you could do something else?

- What would it be?

- How would you go about making it happen?

So, I asked her: if you weren't doing this and you could be doing something else, what would it be? She answered instantly – teaching English as a foreign language. She didn't have to think about it as she'd spent a lot of time thinking about it already. Giving something a lot of thought happens when your (current) work isn't working, or you're unhappy or looking for more fulfilment in your life.

Before the day was over, she shared with me that she'd found an English Teaching course in a month's time and had booked herself on to do it. This was a classic case of 'act boldly, time is limited'; the first rule of 'taming your tiger' – the phrase used by the enigmatic and thought-provoking Jim Lawless.

The cost of doing nothing for this manager would be that she stayed doing what she was doing. That's OK. It's what a lot of people choose to do. Perhaps at a later stage in life they might stop and think to themselves: what if I'd done this? What if I'd done that? Or, as Bronnie Ware discovered, saying to themselves: 'I wish I'd had the courage to live a life true to myself, not the life others expected of me.'

Although this was just one woman's story, I have had similar conversations with countless men and women and every time I see a glimmer of excitement when the person opens up about what they really want to be doing with their life.

Are you plodding?

I'm not a fan of this term, but it's one that is bandied around the corporate world and, for the most part, people know what it is. Businesses will say that they need a percentage of employees who are just happy to plod. By plod they mean that they will come in and do their job and create little fuss. They aren't seen as the superstars or highflyers. They aren't causing the business headaches with performance or attendance issues so, in the manager's mind, they plod.

I don't like the idea that it's OK to leave them to get on with things and pay them little attention. In my experience, people don't plod. People do what they need to do to get on and avoid undue pressure or stress. In most cases, they have figured out how the business operates and recognise how they can get on.

However, those who appear to be doing OK may not be.

If you identify with any of these, then you may be plodding:

- Moaning to partners or colleagues about work.

- Looking for opportunities elsewhere.

- Doing the minimum required.

- Contributing less (than previously).

- Taking on less responsibility (than previously).

- Attending fewer social events.

- Distracted in your work.

- Having 'what if?' thoughts.

Each one of these on their own doesn't amount to much. However, when you start to add them together, that's when you have a challenge on your hands.

The manager who was waiting for retirement

Back in 2009, I was saying my goodbyes to friends and colleagues at M&S Money and about to go it alone and set up my own learning and development consultancy. Having worked for M&S Money for nearly 10 years, I'd come to know a lot of the 1,000 plus people who worked there. I met my first wife there. My first two children had been born during my time there. I'd gone from sales to management and onto learning development, where I discovered my real passion.

Two bits of wisdom stuck out in my mind from everyone I'd said goodbye to. The first was from a senior manager who simply said, 'Good luck. I wish I'd been a little braver when I was younger.' The second came from a fellow manager and it was the one that hit me the hardest. It was not in a personal way but in a way that got me thinking about work differently. When I said my goodbye they responded with, 'All the best, I've only got another 15 years to go until I retire.'

Wow, that got me.

They are still there today! The cost of doing nothing for this manager simply meant that they stayed doing what they were doing.

That's OK, if that's really what your heart wants to do. But if you think you'll be left with regrets, then it's time to reconsider.

'OK' is what a lot of people choose to do. Every one of us will have heard a manager or colleague tell us that 'the grass isn't always greener on the other side.' Without a clear vision of success, at some point all of us will feel frustrated and have a little job dissatisfaction.

Our parents and grandparents would say 'that's life.'

Awareness

Do you recognise any of these issues linked to the so called 'plodders' in your organisation?

- Employee engagement

- Retention

- Productivity

- Absence and/or presenteeism
- Employee wellbeing

Look a little deeper and the issues become far more worrying:

1. Overwork

2. Stress

3. Pain

4. Anxiety

5. Mental health

6. Burnout

Let me dive into these in a bit more detail below.

1. Overwork

a) What is it?

Overwork is nothing new. It's been slowly creeping in for years. At first you don't even see it as overwork.

b) How can you recognise it?

This one is easy to recognise in your life. Perhaps you're getting in early or in the habit of staying after hours. You're likely to be logging back in on your laptop in the evening or checking a few emails over the weekend.

You haven't been helped in this area. It could be argued that companies have been encouraging this practice by providing laptops and mobile phones.

If you find yourself with a manager who is doing the things mentioned here, then the likelihood is that you'll be following their lead. As a leader, it's imperative that you're aware of the behaviours that you are role-modelling; both those conducive to positive wellbeing and those that are destructive.

When I worked at a large mobile phone retailer, I was told on more than one occasion that 'This is a lifestyle and not a career.' One particular senior manager said to me, 'If we need you in at the weekend to write training materials then you will need to come in…'

An article in the *Harvard Business Review* suggests, 'We log too many hours because of a mix of inner drivers, like ambition, machismo, greed, anxiety, guilt, enjoyment, pride, the pull of short-term rewards, a desire to prove we're important, or an overdeveloped sense of duty.'[5]

2. Stress

a) What is it?

This is often a knock-on effect of your overworking, yet you don't always notice the signs. It creeps up on you, like the pressure to hit a deadline or send one more email before shutting off for the evening.

According to the Health and Safety Executive (HSE) in the UK, over 11 million days are lost at work each year because of stress[6]. They point out that stress can happen as a result of workload, lack of training, not enough support and organisational change.

b) How can you recognise it?

There's no doubting that when you're in the 'flow' of getting stuff done, the energy masks any thoughts of you being stressed. Quite the opposite, it manifests itself in the form of a buzz and a last-minute surge towards the completion of a task.

Some people (you may be one of them) would argue that the stress is absolutely necessary and part of their way of working. I'm not disputing that. I too get energised in this way. However, it's important to know the impact of this and the signs of doing too much over a prolonged period of time.

Notice how much energy you have for the other important people or areas of your life when you go through these stressful moments. What's the quality of time like for them and for you? If you're finding yourself with little left to give in terms of energy and attention, it's time to consider if work really is working for you.

I worked with a manager during my time in the Membership department at the Co-Operative. They were relentless with their work. They were first in each morning and last to leave in the evening. They travelled an hour each way and, over time, it started to impact their family life.

They began to look tired and drained, so I asked them one Monday morning if everything was OK. They confided in me that they'd not had a good weekend and spent a large proportion of it arguing with their partner. He was throwing himself into work in order to provide for the family. The stress was mounting and, instead of looking towards home and his family, he was seeking solace by being in work.

3. Pain

a) What is it?

Chronic or persistent pain affects at least 28 million people in the UK[7]. The personal and social costs are enormous. In Europe, the figure reaches €441 billion each year[8]. We are all paying for this in some way: e.g. tax, insurance, allocation of resources. For the individual in pain, life changes, featuring limitations, and suffering that can gather momentum if the pain is misunderstood, ongoing or degenerative.

b) How can you recognise it?

There are many causes of persistent pain. Each person has their own story and their own pain that is inextricably tied to past and present stressors, together with beliefs and expectations.

Both pain and stress are perceived as a result of possible and actual threats. We are then motivated, or even compelled, to act in a way that promotes survival. This is powerful biology at play. Pain is about much more than the person and how they are right now, it includes what they have experienced, and any challenges that they may not have fully processed.

Other things can create internal angst and lead to persistent pain too. For instance, a mismatch of values in the workplace can trigger a biology of protection that rumbles on, causing aches, pains and other common complaints, such as headaches, irritable bowel syndrome, poor sleep and lack of concentration to name but a few.

More learning can be gleaned from reading the work of Specialist Pain Physiotherapist, Richmond Stace, at http://www.specialistpainphysio.com

4. Anxiety

a) What is it?

This is mostly hidden. Certainly, it can be invisible to the untrained eye or manager who hasn't developed their emotional intelligence. However, it can build within you. As it worsens, your heart rate may speed up, your hands may get clammy and the colour of your face can even change subtly.

b) How can you recognise it?

If you're suffering with anxiety at work in any way, you're likely to be doing one of two things: you may be going out of your way to please people and be taking on too much or you may have withdrawn. However, it's much more complex than this in some cases.

A friend of mine actively dresses in a certain way to fit in and not draw attention to herself. Her anxiety prevents her from doing things in work and in life as her thoughts literally stop her in her tracks. She has moments where she appears to be the life and soul of the group, with a real zest for life, but there are other occasions where she simply withdraws and shuts herself away from the world. In part, her anxiety is linked to stress. In part, it's far deeper than that.

After all, the expectations of others (and of yourself) in a working environment can often bring additional stress and pressure that, frankly, isn't helpful.

The old model for success, having a career path and moving up to the next level, is now broken and not fit for purpose. I've seen enough managers and leaders over the years to know that this isn't working. For instance, managers who aren't right for the job being promoted into roles that they cannot perform well. They may not care enough or have the right skills to lead a certain team, yet it's the 'only' way that they can progress.

'To be somebody or to do something. In life there is often a roll call. That's when you will have to make a decision.'

JOHN BOYD

Do you want to 'be someone' in life or do you want to 'do something' with your life? Creating a clear vision of success will help you decide, and you will hear more about this in Chapter 7.

5. Mental health

a) What is it?

Mental health is something we all have (just like physical health) and therefore can be affected either positively or negatively. Your mental health is just as important as your physical health. It's part of your overall wellbeing and, like your physical health, your mental health needs to be worked on.

b) How can you recognise it (when it's not good)?

Physically you may already be looking at diet and exercise. Mentally though, what are you doing? Where in your weekly calendar are you scheduling time to understand some of your thoughts? How are you prioritising things like sleep, mindfulness or disconnecting from technology? Poor mental health has an impact on a number of areas in your life and can lead to an increase in stress levels or anxiety.

It's great to see this getting more attention over the last few years, with the likes of Prince William and Prince Harry supporting the charity Heads Together. There's still a stigma attached to mental health and there's more work that needs to be done.

I wrote an article titled 'Well-being through Well-doing', for *People First* back in February 2019. In that article I stated that, 'Healthy, positive well-being for your organisation is born out of what your people are already doing (or not doing) in their lives and not necessarily from re-working your strategy or adopting the latest trend or fad.'⁹

6. Burnout

a) What is it?

The World Health Organisation (WHO) in 2018 recognised 'burnout as a syndrome linked to chronic work stress.'[10]

b) How can you recognise it?

Burnout has three key elements:

- Feelings of exhaustion.

- Mental detachment from one's job.

- Poorer performance at work.

If you personally don't make a change then it is likely that your current situation will only get worse. The higher you progress, the more you earn and the more that becomes expected of you. The longer you've been in your role, the harder it can be to make a change and the more you start to feel tied down to something making you unhappy.

The areas that I've touched on briefly above aren't independent of one another. They are linked ever so subtly. You already know if you're working too many hours and the impact of doing so. You are likely to also know when stress is having a negative impact on you and your work. You may not be as aware when it comes to how they contribute towards anxiety and poor mental wellbeing.

If you think the change is out of your control, it's not. If you're sitting around waiting for someone to do it for you, they won't. However, in this book I'm going to show you how to make things work, when work isn't working for you.

── Questions to consider ──

1. What does being 'stuck' really feel like? And what have you tried to change so far?

2. Who have you got around your boardroom table that you can talk to? (More on boardroom table later.)

3. Who do you know that isn't 'plodding' but getting on with their life/career?

4. Do you recognise any of the deeper issues (overwork, stress etc.) in your life, and what have you done about them so far?

5. What have you not tried so far that might help you to bring about change?

CHAPTER 3

MY STORY

'Act boldly, time is limited.'

JIM LAWLESS – TAMING TIGERS

T hose words have served me well in my life over the last 10 years and allowed me to do many things when I too realised that work wasn't working. However, before then my life was a very different story. Unbeknown to me, for a large proportion of my life I'd been living with an unconscious thought that I was going to die aged 34.

There was no logic to that fear, none that I can see as I reflect through my current lens of life. However, as I got closer and closer to my 34th birthday, I couldn't explain some of my thoughts and behaviours. I'd become withdrawn from everybody: my wife, family, friends and colleagues. I was unable to articulate or share my thoughts; the fear was real, and it was consuming me.

My dad

Our dad was hardworking, relaxed and fun. Dan (my brother) and I would sit on the stairs with our legs through the bannisters and wave him off to work some mornings. We'd sit on the sofa with him and watch TV whilst he sat and smoked his pipe. As a family we'd go for walks in the park that our house backed onto or we'd play in the garden with the dog.

Our school was at the top of a hill, to which we walked most days. We enjoyed our time there, and the opportunity to play with our friends. Mum worked part time at the school, I suspect more to keep an eye on us rather than anything else. Occasionally, we'd see other family members and sometimes spend some time with our grandparents. We had a normal life, as far as we could tell. That was until Dad became ill.

At five (Dan) and six (me) you don't really understand what's going on. You just notice things, like Dad not going to work or playing with us very much. All of a sudden, the house seemed to get busier and we had friends of Mum and Dad's, and uncles and aunties visiting. Each of them was taking the time to see if we were OK and playing with us.

Although we didn't know it, Dad had cancer and he wasn't in a good place. He'd become weak and he was battling for his life. Even a hug with us required all his effort.

It felt like one day he was there and the next he was gone.

I don't know where Dan and I had been for the morning or who we had been with, but we came home to a house full of family. Every single one of them was dressed in black (which looked odd), speaking quietly to one another and trying to force a smile for us.

Mum and our grandad took us into the front room and told us that Dad had died and gone to heaven. Time stopped. Everything was a blur. Both of us burst into tears.

I could see Mum and Grandad were crying too. I didn't know what to think or say. Dan said something, but I don't recall what it was – he was always the 'chatty' one – but I was numb. We went back into the lounge and joined the rest of the family. At some point everybody left, and it was just the three of us.

Dad was 34 years old.

I still struggle to comprehend that now, over 35 years later. He was young. Too young. The number 34 was to stay with me for many years.

Within 18 months of Dad dying, the three of us had moved in with mum's brother Brian and sister-in-law Linda and left our family home. They didn't have children at the time and for a short while that became our home, until our own house was built next door. That wasn't the only change though. On the advice and recommendation of our grandparents, we'd also moved from our local school.

At six (Dan) and seven (me), in September 1984, we arrived at Rydal School in Colwyn Bay, North Wales; it was a boarding school an hour away from Mum and where our home was. I've spoken many times to those closest to me about that first day/night at boarding school. We weren't meant to be there. It wasn't our choice; we didn't even know what 'boarding' actually meant.

Then we heard those words from our mum, 'Right boys, it's time for us to go now. We will see you at the end of October for half-term break.'

I remember asking Mum what she meant and why we weren't going home with her. I could see it was hard for her too, as she tried to fight back the tears and put on a brave face for her boys. The matron, Miss Galbraith, held our hands and tried to reassure us and Mum that we'd be OK. Two senior boys who we'd never met duly arrived from nowhere to launch us onto their shoulders and carry us outside to wave goodbye to Mum.

There wasn't a dry eye in the dormitory that night, or for the subsequent nights that followed. There were 11 boys brought together from different backgrounds and a variety of family circumstances. This would be 'home' for us for the next 10 years, going to our actual home only for half-term or end of term holidays. Ten years when you're six and seven felt like a lifetime. We arrived as boys and left as young men.

Over those 10 years, I thought a lot about Dad, and it was during this time that I first harboured thoughts about dying at a young age as well. I never shared them with anyone, not even my brother.

The family didn't talk about Dad as it upset everyone. Mum had met another man and started to move on with her life. Ken, or Kenny as we called him, was brilliant with us right from day one. He called us 'lads' and generally gave us lots of freedom to play and behave as lads do. Ken served in the Royal Marines and so discipline and manners were important. He didn't try to take the place of Dad; he was his own man and just helped where he could.

As I grew older, though, I wanted to know what had happened to Dad. But I felt like I had no one to talk to. The family had become a bit disjointed and I withdrew. I started to believe that I would die at 34 and carried the idea with me every day.

Fast forward to September 2008 (aged 32)

I joined M&S Money in 2000, having spent five years working in a number of roles in hospitality in a number of four-star hotels. This had provided me with lots of experience of working with others and grounded me in the art of customer service and how to deal with 'in the moment' feedback.

The focus and emphasis placed on 'getting it right' first time has remained with me through my career. Being able to sense when customers are happy and unhappy has also helped me when it comes to being intuitive around others.

I steadily moved up the ranks, so to speak, joining M&S Money as a salesperson before becoming a team manager. Whilst I saw that work as a means to an end, I had aspirations and a desire to be able to help others.

After a few years, I was 'approached' at the photocopier and asked if I'd ever consider working in learning and development. I'd never trained anyone before, but strangely I knew I could do it. I said yes and within a few months found myself in the beautiful Mumbai in India, training 150 people. That experience had a significant impact on my life, and each year I took on more of the opportunities that would allow me to be me and allow me to shine.

You see, I had an ego, an ego that was driving me. Coupled with my fear of dying (relatively soon), this influenced me to be all kinds of things to anyone and everyone. I couldn't see it then. That kind of awareness would only come later on.

I had ambitions to go it alone and set up my own business. If my time was indeed to be limited, then something had to change to make this happen. Indeed, change was about to happen. Our daughter, Becky, had been born in 2004 and the arrival of our second child, Alex, was imminent.

Work had begun to feel like, well, just work. The excitement of travelling to India or working on big roadshow events at Old Trafford and Wembley were mere memories in the distance. I had a well-paid job, working for a very good employer. My boss got me and what drove me and encouraged me to do what I did best.

I knew I was getting bored, and in my conversations with others I knew they were bored too. Strangely (or deliberately), I'd gravitated towards people who were unsure, bored, frustrated or wanting a change in their lives. These conversations were pointing to the same thing for me: work wasn't working anymore. I'd slipped into the daily grind outlined in Chapter 1 and, more importantly, I no longer had a clear vision of success to guide me.

Outside of work, I'd become withdrawn. I had become quieter at home and was drinking more. I wasn't the same 'life and soul of the party' guy that I had been previously. Life felt serious and I'd never been one to fully 'grow up'. Family and friends were as supportive and encouraging as ever; I couldn't have asked for anything more. They weren't the problem. It was me.

I reverted to my childhood default state of keeping quiet and not being able to talk. My family didn't talk about feelings ever. I know this is common in a lot of families too.

I'd lost the ability to open up and share. Who do you share those innermost thoughts with?

I'd found myself being the 'listener' for others, but I didn't feel that I had anyone in my life to turn to and share my feelings with. In hindsight I did, I just didn't know how to have those conversations.

Back to September 2008

My boss gave a team briefing and shared with us that she was bringing in an external consultant by the name of Kirsty Mac to do some communication and mindset training. We'd seen a lot of consultants come into M&S Money over the years, with varying degrees of success, and this seemed like just another one in a long list. Little did I know that this time it would be the cause of a different line of thinking. She had arranged a taster day for a small number of the team to test the materials and gauge our responses about doing more work.

Thirty minutes into the taster day and I was mesmerised. I couldn't believe it myself either. Kirsty has a way of connecting with each and every person in the room. She listened to me and started to understand me.

I'd become a bit of a cynic about external consultants, in part because I'd seen so many over the previous five years and also because of my jealousy and desire to want to be one! However, something happened during the morning that set off lightbulbs in my mind. My strongly held views of external consultants, which I was desperate to hold onto, was being challenged – in a good way.

My boss asked me at lunch for my thoughts and intimated that she was looking at bringing Kirsty back in a couple of weeks. It was a resounding yes from me.

My thoughts then turned to the imminent arrival of our second child, Alex. He was due to be born around 14th September and my paternity would be for one week. I didn't want to miss this training! I spoke to my wife that evening and we wondered if my boss might let me take my paternity over two weeks instead of one so that I could attend the training.

It was a yes from my boss.

That would mean attending four days of training over two weeks. As strange as it may sound, those four days changed my life. They changed my thinking radically.

My personal beliefs and values had been challenged and all in a positive way. I'd held one belief for a long time: 'Good guys don't get on.' In turn, this had led me to believe that the only way to get on in life was to be an arse! Similarly, I have a personal value around making a difference, which I still do today. I started to see how I might be able to make a bigger difference in the world outside of M&S Money. I'd become aware of my beliefs and values on a much deeper level.

I went home each evening excited – and also mentally drained. I can't recall another time in my life where learning had had such a profound effect; it had got to me.

Everything about losing Dad and the thoughts I'd been carrying around with me all of my life were circulating around in my head. These were coupled with my new thoughts:

- What if?

- What next?

- Where do I go from here?

In truth, I didn't know any of the answers at that point.

I'd go into the training and ask lots of questions, then during the breaks, I'd ask Kirsty more questions. I was searching for answers. In the evening, I'd talk the day through with my wife at the time, Jo, and try to make sense of it all. The next day, I'd repeat the same process. Four days wasn't enough. I still had answers to find and questions to ask, but time was against me.

I'd suddenly become curious about doing something different. These thoughts and feelings left me wanting to discover more.

I reached out to Kirsty once more; I got the impression she knew I would! Anyhow, come November I found myself in Glasgow, working with Kirsty once more. That week, spent with 10 other people who I'd never met before in my life, changed my path forever.

Through sharing and listening to others share their stories, I realised what was holding me back. It was me. I realised that I wasn't happy doing what I was doing, but I thought I was. My job was easy and fun, but I'd done everything I could possibly do within the learning and development team.

The fact was, I'd been going through the motions and the same daily grind that I described earlier in the book. I felt stuck and I didn't have the confidence or belief to change. Not until... August 2009.

That was the year I was turning 34.

Looking back, I don't think there was a week that went by when I didn't consider the impact and enormity of this. Once more, I made a decision, a decision that would lead me down another path. I decided to go back to the scene of my most recent learning and my discoveries about myself – Glasgow.

The first week of a two-week programme got to me. I shared, I cried, I shared some more, and I cried some more. I had a lot of alone time. In the evenings, I'd go to the pub and talk with complete strangers. By the end of the week, I felt good for having gone through the experience, but I also felt anxious about October.

Choose today,

choose now.

I was returning for week two and it was my birthday at the start of the week. I honestly didn't know how to feel as I boarded the train and headed to Glasgow once more. My family, as always, were supportive and loving.

I arrived at my hotel and there was a card for me. On opening it, I discovered that it was a birthday card from the other members of my group and Kirsty. The message read:

'Happy birthday and welcome to your 35th year.'

Talk about a life-changing moment; I couldn't believe it. I reread that message over and over and over again, tears of joy rolling down my cheeks. Here I was, miles away from my family and worried about what the future might hold, and by the words of one message, my life changed forever.

By the end of that week my beliefs had started to change, and I had a new confidence. I left with a clear plan to bring about change in my life; I had a new energy, focus and determination. Three months later, my journey was headed down a new path.

Along this path, I've been able to help many others face up to the reality of their life and go about making changes. What are you waiting for? You don't have to be one of those people who say, 'One day I'll do this' or 'One day I'll do that.' Work hasn't been working for you for some time, and I'm offering to show you ways to make it work once more. It's not as hard as you think; you just need to get started.

Like I did.

Take the plunge and take back control. Find some inspiration within this book and take on board some of the lessons that I've learned from some amazing and generous people.

Choose today, choose now.

— Questions to consider —

1. What's holding you back?

2. What would 'acting boldly' look like for you?

3. If not now, when (will you start to bring about changes in your life)?

4. What if you couldn't fail... what would you have a go at?

5. How do you want the next 10 years of 'your story' to look different to the last 10?

CHAPTER 4

ON YOUR MARKS, GET SET...

*'If you change the way you look at things,
the things you look at change.'*

WAYNE DYER

Fixed vs growth mindset

I f the mind is willing, then the body will follow. In today's world we talk about a growth mindset and a fixed mindset. A growth mindset is your springboard to embracing change and adapting in the future. A closed mindset will get you right back to where you currently are. For want of a better description, if you're 'oohing and aahing' about making a change, then there's a good chance that you're talking yourself out of it already.

I hear these phrases all the time, and perhaps the little voice in your head is saying some of them to you right now:

- It's not that bad really.

- I'm OK.

- Things could be worse.

- I don't want to create a fuss.

- I've got my appraisal at the end of the month and I'll do it then.

- What could I do?

- How would I even start?

- I've never done that before.

- One day I'll do it.

- When I get time.

To put it nicely, you're simply procrastinating at this stage. You know that. What you may not have considered is the length of time that you've been procrastinating or putting something off for. Here's a simple example to illustrate the point.

The manager who wanted to skydive

Back in 2012 I was delivering a leadership programme to leaders in the retail part of a well-known mobile phone business. Part of this leadership programme focused on coaching.

One of the managers in the group was very forthcoming and shared that he'd 'always wanted to jump out of an aeroplane.' When I questioned him a little further, he'd actually had this idea and been thinking about it for eight years!

'Wow!' I said. 'Eight years you've wanted to jump out of an aeroplane, and you haven't done it yet. How come?'

He proceeded to share the many reasons why he'd not got around to doing it. I could see from his body language that he was a little disappointed.

'How would it feel to do that jump?' I asked him.

He paused for a moment to consider this. His eyes were going everywhere as he took himself to that place and imagined jumping. He came alive and was animated as he described passionately his feelings.

'Wow,' I said. 'But here's the thing; you haven't really wanted to jump out of an aeroplane. If you had, at some point during the last eight years you'd have done it.'

Imagine his response to me (in front of 15 other managers). I let him vent his frustration as he defended his reasons why he hadn't. The group sat silently, unsure what to say or where to look.

—❝—

Life passes us by

if we're not paying

attention.

—❞—

When he calmed down, I thanked him for sharing his example of a goal he wanted to achieve. And I thanked him for allowing me to question and challenge his thoughts.

His story could have easily been a carbon copy of someone else in the group on that day. Let me break down the stages:

1. He had an idea of a goal that he wanted to achieve.

2. He had started with a thought and perhaps a good intention.

3. Sadly, he didn't do anything with it.

4. His vision of success wasn't clear enough.

5. He got distracted or more important things took his attention.

6. His life took over.

Life passes us by if we're not paying attention. If something is important enough, then it gets our attention. If it's not, it doesn't.

Something changed in his mindset during the morning of that day. He made a conscious choice to do something different, something that he'd not done up to that point.

After lunch he returned to the training room with a huge smile on his face. He had some news and he couldn't wait to share it. I waited for everyone to return from lunch before I turned to the manager and asked him if he had something he wanted to share with the group.

His words were: 'I've done it. I've spoken to my wife. I've made some enquiries. I'm going to be jumping out of an aeroplane on "x" Sunday in June this year. I know the exact field that I'll be landing in. Oh, and I'm going to do it for "x" charity.'

The rest of the group applauded and there were some high-fives going on as well. Everyone in the group offered to sponsor him. He was looking pretty pleased with himself and his actions.

I asked him, 'What changed?'

'You were right,' he said. 'I'd been making up excuses and convincing myself that one day I would do it. It hadn't become important enough for me, until today.'

There are many reasons why we choose to procrastinate, and some of it is down to self-preservation. A protective measure, if you like, to keep us safe.

A question for you to consider is: how is this serving you? If it's serving you well, then carry on. If it's not serving you well, it's time to make that change.

How your mind works

To help you get more clarity on this, I want to share some thoughts from Prof Steve Peters, author of the excellent book, *The Chimp Paradox*.

He talks in his book (and at an event in January 2020) about the mind being made up of three separate brains:

1. The human

2. The chimp

3. The computer

Briefly

The chimp brain is the emotional part of our brain, and it's a separate entity to you. There's no point arguing with a chimp. It's driven by emotional needs such as self-esteem. The emotional need (from the chimp) will keep on kicking you until you deal with it (using the human brain). The chimp looks at the world as win or lose.

The human brain tries to reason with the chimp, only you can't reason with the chimp. With the human brain there's no win or lose, just solutions. The human brain deals with facts, logic and reasoning. This can't control the chimp, but you can manage your emotions coming from the chimp by programming the computer part of the brain.

The computer brain is where the programming takes place. It's a storage area for our thoughts and behaviours. The computer stores information that the chimp or the human has put into it. Our hardwiring is in here, making it a challenge (though not impossible) to make changes. It uses this information to act in an automatic way.

The trouble, for all of us, is that the human part of the brain is unable to talk directly with the chimp part of the brain. Why? Because the chimp runs on emotions and doesn't listen to logic. Try it.

Think of a change that you want to make in your life right now. Or, as an example, let's look at switching off from social media in the evening. What is the human (logical) brain saying? Something like: it's a good idea. It makes sense. I know I should do this. I could get lots done in the evening.

Now, what is the chimp (emotional) brain saying? Something like: oh, but I'm important. I need to share my message. This is a good use of my time. Notice the difference?! There's a good chance that you've found yourself in similar situations many times over in your life. What hope do you have? Well, there is plenty.

I'll continue with the theme offered by the chimp paradox for a moment. The chimp part of the brain is influenced by the computer part of the brain. Remember that the computer part of the brain is the storage area, our hardwiring. New thoughts are added all the time and, over time, they can become part of our hardwiring.

You've probably been aware of this or known this for a while. What's not always been helpful is the theory of how long it takes to learn a new behaviour before it becomes a habit. According to Maxwell Maltz (a plastic surgeon in the 1950s), it takes about 21 days for a patient to get used to a new situation.[11] In the 1960s he published that theory and his other thoughts on behavioural change in a book called *Psycho-Cybernetics* (audiobook). The book went on to become a blockbuster hit, selling more than 30 million copies.

For years we've been told it takes 21 days to form a new habit by self-help gurus, including Zig Ziglar, Brian Tracy and Tony Robbins – 21 days being short enough to inspire and long enough to believe.

However, a study by Phillippa Lally (a health psychology researcher at University College London) found that, 'On average, it takes more than two months before a new behaviour becomes automatic — 66 days to be exact[12].'

In Lally's study, it took anywhere from 18 days to 254 days for people to form a new habit. James Clear also writes about this in his excellent book, *Atomic Habits*. He suggests that, 'If you want to set your expectations appropriately, the truth is that it will probably take you anywhere from two months to eight months to build a new behaviour into your life — not 21 days.' Therefore, you must expect to be rubbish at first (learning), steadily improving (more learning and practise) before you become proficient (through even more learning and practise).

Ready to be challenged?

If you are, then the opportunities can be limitless for you. Your progress comes from being uncomfortable. By definition, the comfort zone is comfortable, but it doesn't allow you to develop or grow. Be mindful of what society and/or convention says. Some of the stuff getting your attention is a deliberate distraction. There's a lot of 'noise' that won't be serving you well.

Remember the teacher or manager who said you couldn't do something, but you did it anyway? Let those examples provide hope and use the tools within this book to propel you to where you want to get to next.

— Questions to consider —

1. What are some of your frequent reasons for procrastinating? Write them down and ask yourself 'Why is this the case?' with each of them.

2. Which of the goals on your bucket list have you been putting off the longest? Ask yourself if you still want to achieve them.

3. In which situations can you see your 'chimp' taking over and preventing you from acting?

4. If you were to start by spending 1% of your day (14.4 minutes) doing something different or new, what would it be?

5. What's stopping you from starting today and doing that for at least 66 days?

CHAPTER 5

OBSTACLES ARE PART OF THE WAY

'There is no good or bad without us, there is only perception. There is the event itself and the story we tell ourselves about what it means.'

RYAN HOLIDAY – *THE OBSTACLE IS THE WAY*

Let's be clear. Meaningful, lasting change takes time. We've already discovered in the previous chapter that it takes longer (than 21 days) for us to form a new habit. Perhaps longer than you previously realised.

Life hacks and shortcuts aren't what I'm providing in this book. There are tools that you can start to implement quickly or start to use straightaway. The basis of what is provided in this book is centred and focused on empowering and enabling you for the long game. The long game will deliver more lasting change and enable you to work through many obstacles along the way.

Patience is required for this journey as you'll be faced with temptations at every corner. Temptations come in the form of quick fixes and shortcuts. Even distraction will do its best to alter your path and convince you to give in to short-term success. You will become stronger with each new obstacle faced, and you will become better equipped in the longer term to overcome new challenges.

Marcus Aurelius reminds us that 'the mind adapts and converts to its own purpose the obstacle to our acting', 'the impediment to action advances action', and 'what stands in the way becomes the way.'

Take comfort from this. Your obstacles don't have to be blockers. Start to view them differently and notice what happens. See them as part of the journey, and challenges along the way.

Let's call them what they are: fears. These are the most common fears that I've helped clients work through:

1. Fear of change (new, unknown)

2. Fear of failure (self-preservation, ego)

3. Fear of security (survival, status)

4.   Fear of being you (your identity, vulnerability)

I suspect that, for most of you reading this book, some of these fears have already stopped you from making a change in your life.

Fear

Fear is OK, but it's important to recognise when fear is working positively for you or negatively against you. Without it we would find ourselves in real trouble. When you fear something, your mind instinctively moves into fight, flight or freeze mode. You confront it and fight it. You take flight and run away from it. Or you simply freeze and hope it'll pass quickly.

In each of the sections on fear, I'll provide a brief suggestion for how to overcome each particular fear. The suggestions are brief and effective. I've seen them work successfully with individuals in every organisation I've worked with.

I like Caroline Paul's view on fear. She's not against fear. She thinks fear is definitely important, and it's there to keep us safe. She does, however, think that some people give it too much priority. For her, fear is one of many things going on in a particular situation. Other thoughts and emotions taking place may include, anticipation, exhilaration, focus, confidence and fun. She likes to ask herself the question, how much priority am I going to give this? As you may have guessed, she is all for being brave and courageous.

Caroline Paul is the author of four books, including *The Gutsy Girl*, a *New York Times* bestseller.

1. Fear of change

Why do we fear change?

We fear change because it upsets our status quo. It challenges us to consider new thoughts, ideas and processes that we may not know or be comfortable with. Change is new, and whilst new may be exciting for some, for others it's daunting. Some change requires new learning and not everyone is comfortable being a beginner again.

When do we fear change?

We fear change most when it challenges us outwardly in front of others. This is happening more than organisations either realise or like to think. The majority of employees won't speak up or ask for help when going through change.

Why? They simply don't want to appear to be incompetent in front of colleagues or management as it would cause them embarrassment and potentially lead to anxiety. One of the common models to consider is the Elisabeth Kübler-Ross Change Curve.

Elisabeth Kübler-Ross Change Curve

The Kübler-Ross Change Curve is also known as the Five Stages of Grief. Whilst the loss of a loved one, for example, is clearly different to experiencing change in the workplace, it has been proven that there are similarities in terms of emotions that we might experience.

This is a model consisting of the various levels or stages of emotions that are experienced by a person who is soon going to approach death. It was introduced in her book *On Death and Dying*, which was published in 1969.

The five stages are:

1. Denial

2. Anger

3. Bargaining

4. Depression

5. Acceptance

This has been adapted many times and so you may be familiar with a slightly different version.

How it's supposed to work

The organisation announces that there's a change coming. So, what happens is that you deny all knowledge of the said change *(denial)* about to take place. You show some frustration to your colleagues *(anger)* or the people responsible for the change. Then you go home and share some more anger, sometimes saying to your spouse or partner, 'You'll never guess what...'

When you're back in work, you start to explore ways to put this off or delay *(bargaining)* the change from impacting you. You move towards others who think and feel the same and you bitch and moan about the good old days, generally feeling pretty shitty about everything *(depression)*. Then, as if by magic, you start to come around to the idea of the change *(acceptance)*.

At each stage, you'll find yourself being cajoled and encouraged along the way. Or sold the utopia of what a great place it will be once this change has been implemented. You get the idea, even if it's being facilitated slightly differently within your organisation.

Making it personal

Most change models will help facilitate a change and deliver a certain amount of success. I get why they are used and referred to as organisations are often looking to bring about a big change. I've used them myself and experienced them as an employee.

What they can lack, in many cases, is a personal touch. How do you make it more personal for everyone? What is the impact to each person?

Those people with reservations or hesitations may or may not share them, as mentioned earlier in this chapter. A question for organisations to consider is: how can they create an environment where everyone feels comfortable enough to share their questions and reservations?

A fear of change can be worked through effectively if the working environment allows us to feel comfortable enough to do this openly. Where we don't feel that our judgment or opinion might be held against us, and an environment where concerns (or fears) that are raised can be talked through. In these circumstances, we're more likely to share our views and support the change to happen.

For some of you, you'll also have a personal fear of change and not just the change imposed or brought about by the organisation that you're working for. This is a fear of a self-driven change that you want to bring about. This can include that role that you want to apply for internally or the department you'd like to work in.

If you make that move (or change), what if it goes badly wrong or doesn't work out? The self-talk says, 'What if I'm useless at it?' Maybe it's best to stay doing what you're doing as you're good at it.

How can this fear hold us back?

The fear of change, if you allow it to, will hold you back, but for how long? That's up to you. It can lead to a feeling of paralysis – a feeling of being stuck and unable to move forward, whilst getting more and more frustrated with where you are.

How to tackle this fear

1. Talk to someone else about it.

2. Share your thoughts on what's holding you back when it comes to making a change.

3. Work through the exercises later in this book around vision and values.

These will give you greater clarity on what it is you're wanting to change and work towards. They will also ensure that you have the right people in place to support you with any change.

2. Fear of failure

Why do we fear failure?

We fear failure because we have failed at some point(s) in our life and we didn't like it. We did not enjoy the experience at all. By definition, it's a harsh teacher and one that few of us want to repeat or see again. Indeed, failure isn't seen as cool and as a result is seldom celebrated.

When do we fear failure?

This is something each and every one of us has had experience with at some point in our lives. In fact, for some people this is happening every day. For any one of us, it can become ingrained in our mind and talk to us every day. It's the voice that says: *Are you sure you want to do that? What if you fail or it doesn't work out? What will others think or say?*

Take your mind back to when you were in school, aged between six and eight. This might not be a good place for you to go, but there's a point I'm going to prove shortly.

The scenario

I want you to look back on a time when a teacher asked a question in class (a class of between 20 and 30 kids). You put up your hand, as many other kids did, to answer the question. Now, kids at this age are usually excitable and on the edge of their seats, wanting to be chosen to answer the teacher's question. They might even have been shouting out, 'Pick me, Miss Rowlands!' (other teachers are available).

The teacher's eyes fall on you and then it's up to you to provide the answer in front of the whole class. Composing yourself, you share your answer with great gusto, only for it to be incorrect.

If you have experienced this in your life (not just in school) then you know how it feels. At school, though, kids aged six, seven and eight are generally brutal and very unforgiving. That one moment in front of the class, you play over and over and over many times in your mind. Why? Because you got it wrong.

It may have been the first time you got something wrong, but you (and others) forget about the many times you've got things right. Some people carry this fear of failure with them into the next class, the next meeting or the next presentation. The result of this is that you don't give it your best because you're already worried and consumed with how others will respond to you. Or in some cases you hide behind an ego and look for self-preservation in the face of others.

How a fear of failure can hold you back

Failure is often where we learn the most, myself included. It's harsh and it's cruel, but sometimes it's unavoidable.

Michael Jordan (greatest basketball player of all time!) is often quoted when it comes to failure, saying, 'I've missed more than 9,000 shots in my career, lost more than 300 games. Twenty-six times I've been trusted to take the game winning shot and missed. I've failed over and over and over in my life and that is why I succeed.'

The reality here is that you have a choice.

a) Carry on doing what you've done before and thus avoid any chance of failure.

b) Have a go and see how you get on, knowing that if you fail you will have that learning to help you in the future.

I've shared on numerous occasions that I failed first time around in business. In fact, you could say I failed miserably, but it's because I failed then that I was able to succeed the second time, when that opportunity presented itself to me again.

How to tackle this fear

1.   Choose option B over A and see how you get on.

2. Learn to use the 'if this' strategy. In his book *Achieve the Impossible*, Professor Greg Whyte talks about adopting 'if this' strategies. If you work out what might go wrong in advance, then you can formulate an 'if this' strategy to counter that particular obstacle.

One example relates to what to do if you don't get an interview for a job role that you'd like to do. If this happens, you could approach the Hiring Manager for feedback and you could speak to the Department Manager and express your interest in future roles. If this happens, you could ask to spend time in that department getting to know others and understand more about the work they do.

3. Fear of security

Why do we fear a loss of security?

We fear a loss of what we have because it's ours and we've worked hard for it. As human beings we are not programmed particularly well to give up things or elements of our life. We attach emotion and thoughts to what we have and what is ours, to lose security or status in front of others causes shame and embarrassment, or so we tell ourselves.

When do we fear a loss of security?

This is something that might not be obvious to see at first. Again, we all experience this at some points in our lives, as you go through your career, this will become either more or less apparent.

Think back to getting your first job. Having money in your bank account and being able to treat yourself or show off to your mates.

Think back to the probation period when you'd got a new job or a received a promotion. You would have been giving it everything to prove you could do the job and get the role permanently.

Now, think back to when you didn't have a job, or perhaps you have experienced being made redundant, as I have. All of a sudden, you've lost your 'status' and it becomes all about survival. There's an expectation and sometimes desperation for you to find another job!

Knowing and having that security allows you to survive and, in a few cases, thrive. You can enjoy the trappings that your career and work afford you. Perhaps you've made a career out of doing enough to survive and progress, accepting promotions and different responsibilities along the way. On the other hand, perhaps this approach has held you back!

How a fear of loss of security can hold you back

You see, sometimes a fear of losing your security can stop you from saying no, like avoiding saying 'no' to doing extra work or taking on other responsibilities. Or saying 'yes' to becoming a manager, when really you don't want to manage other people

I've looked in the mirror
and know what I am and
what I am not.

and would prefer to stay in sales. Or staying in one company for 5, 10, 15 or more years, because actually you were too scared to leave or walk away from what you already had.

Like any fear, a fear of security can be worked through in a similar way to the others discussed so far. Now that might be a little bold or courageous for you. As Ant Middleton (former SAS Commander and author of *First Man In: Leading From the Front*) writes, 'I've looked in the mirror and know what I am and what I am not.'

How to tackle this fear

1. Ask yourself what is keeping you where you are right now. Understand and talk through what's holding you back. Be honest with yourself.

I'll show you later, in Part Two of the book, some strategies for getting clearer on your vision in addition to which values can drive you towards achieving that. For now, allow yourself some time to reflect on the obstacles you face on your pathway towards where you want to be in life.

4. Fear of being you

Why do we fear being ourselves?

For the large majority of our lives, we have been performing roles. From a child through to a teenager and then into employment, we have been conditioned (in many ways) to fit in and conform. The thing is that we're all unique and designed to stand out in our own way. We fear being ourselves, because in most cases, we don't know who our true self is, and we live in a world where we are judged 24/7 for everything.

When do we fear being ourselves?

Who doesn't experience this fear at some point in their lives?

Think back to Bronnie Ware and the top five regrets of the dying:

> *'I wish I'd had the courage to live a life true to myself, not the life others expected of me.'*

Family plays a part in this, as does education. Even the organisations that you choose to work for.

In your early (formative) years you're told to do this and do that, whilst often being encouraged to fit in and be like others. In school it takes a certain amount of courage to stray outside of the 'cool gang' or too far away from the classmates who have some influence over followers. Early on in your career, it's often frowned upon if you challenge or question.

Outside of the home, school and business, society in general doesn't help. The focus, and therefore what you're conditioned to do, is to strive for success in your life. Achieve one goal, then move onto the next one. Work towards one promotion and then strive for the next one.

If you're not careful, though, all your goals and successes will have been for someone else or for some organisation.

It's no wonder that people suffer with what is described as a 'mid-life crisis'. This happens at a certain point (usually around the age of 40), when you look back at what you've achieved in your life and, for some reason, feel disappointed.

How a fear of being you can hold you back

When you can't be you, you'll default to being whatever other people want or need you to be. You'll strive to fit in at all costs because the opposite of standing out holds little appeal to you. You become reliant on others to make decisions for you or to provide suggestions as to what you should do in any given situation. If you want confirmation of this, simply look at any of the social media platforms on any day and see how many people are asking strangers for help!

How to tackle this fear

This is perhaps the hardest fear to overcome, but it's definitely possible. Although it is one that I like to call a 'work in progress' as there's definitely no hack or quick fix to this one.

This doesn't have to be the case.

1. How you overcome your fear of being you, is to start by being you. Start by understanding who you really are and what you represent.

2. Then you should look at what's important to you in terms of your life. Work out what will drive you towards achieving what it is you truly want to achieve. Remember all of your fears and challenges are mere obstacles in the way. Like any obstacle, they can be moved or moved around. In the forthcoming chapters I'll provide you with the tools you need and some more inspiring stories to help bring about change in your life, so that you can start making work, work for you.

3. At whatever stage in your life or career you can look back and feel proud. Proud in respect to the person you are. And proud in the decisions you have made and the actions you have taken.

The parable of the two wolves is a Cherokee legend

It illustrates the most important battle of our lives – the one between our good and bad thoughts. Here is how the story goes:

A grandfather is talking with his grandson. The grandfather says, 'In life, there are two wolves inside of us that are always at battle. One is a good wolf, which represents things like kindness, bravery and love. The other is a bad wolf, which represents things like greed, hatred and fear.' The grandson stops and thinks about it for a minute and then he looks up at his grandfather and says, 'Grandfather, which wolf will win?'

The grandfather replies, 'The one you feed.'

As Kanye West says: 'I got to cheer for me before anyone else can cheer for me.'

— Questions to consider —

1. Which fear is holding you back the most? Be honest with yourself and write down the reasons why.

2. For each of the reasons why, write down one scary thing you could do to counter that fear.

3. What obstacles do you perceive to be in the way of you making change(s)?

4. Who do you know (in your circle or through another connection) who has overcome similar obstacles?

5. What action(s) can you take now to overcome or move past an obstacle?

CHAPTER 6

THE MODEL – THE 6 Vs

'If you chase two rabbits,
you will catch neither.'

CONFUCIUS

'Action may not always bring happiness, but
there is no happiness without action.'

BENJAMIN DISRAELI

Introduction to the 6 Vs

As you have seen already, bringing about change in your life requires a number of things to happen. It is why, sadly, most New Year's resolutions are destined to fail, and it is also why a large proportion of people will give in along the way and revert back to how things were previously.

Some people are looking for a quick fix or a life hack, but that's not what I'm sharing or advocating here. The stories I've shared so far, and the stories to come, all have one thing in common: they understand the long game and follow a process to achieve the change they want to bring about.

Ryan Holiday refers to 'the process' in *The Obstacle is the Way* as: 'When we get distracted, the process is the helpful, if occasionally bossy voice in our head, the voice that demands we take responsibility and ownership.'

In the previous chapter, I talked about fear and how it can hold you back. What I'm about to share is a model that can set you free from the daily grind and propel you to a place in your life that, up until now, has been reserved for your dreams and moments of your imagination. If you commit yourself to following the model, you will undoubtedly overcome and lose some of your previous fears along the way.

This model works – I've been refining and using this process and model for the last 10 years. In that time, I've seen plenty of success along the way. I've seen people who have been stuck for years in a role break free from the daily grind and tell me they've reignited their career as a result of following this model. I've watched retail managers achieve promotion after promotion and become area and divisional leaders having followed this model. I've witnessed boards of directors transform their own style and approach to leadership as a result of personally choosing to go through this model, having observed the changes seen in the people attending my programmes.

Trust in it. Lean into it. Depend on it.

The model is the 6 Vs

The 6 Vs model and process will take you to a place in your life where you'll be showing up at your work instead of turning up to work every day.

The 6 Vs are:

- Vision

- Values

- View

- Vehicle

- Valour

- Voice

Each of the 6 Vs represents an important part of the process as you bring about change in your life. This process moves you from where you are today to a place where you'll be energised and motivated by the work you do. You'll be fulfilled by what you are achieving each month and quarter, and you will be able to see clear progression towards your overall goal. Finally, you'll feel in control – the master of your destiny rather than just being led by what your managers/employers want you to do. You will feel more confident with your decision making and not afraid to speak up.

In the following chapters you'll begin to see the importance of them all together and what happens when one or more of these Vs is missing or has not been clearly articulated and worked through. If the exercises leave you wanting more, then you can sign up to the 6 Steps to Achieving Your Vision of Success online programme, that I personally facilitate. That will offer a deep dive into each of the 6 Vs, where you'll also experience some coaching from me and a member of the team.

Prepare to do the work and you will be rewarded. You will make work work for you. In fact, once you make the changes to your own life, you'll feel empowered to want to share this with your friends, colleagues and family.

In brief

- Your vision is about having a clear vision of success to focus on.

- Your values are what drive you to get out of bed each day.

- Your view refers to where you are now (in your current job) in relation to your vison and values.

- Your vehicle is how you create an environment for change.

- Your valour focuses on ensuring success by identifying blockers and being courageous.

- Your voice is how to share your thoughts and build your support team.

My inspiration for the model

The inspiration for the model has come from thousands of hours of reading, watching and listening to:

- Books

- Articles

- Blog posts

- Ted talks

- YouTube videos

- Webinars

- Events

- Skype conversations

- Zoom discussions

Honestly, though, these are just a fraction of where the inspiration has come from. The real inspirations and light-bulb moments have come from working with hundreds of other people. Sometimes it has been completed in training rooms, through coaching conversations, or by observing people in general, but it has mostly been developed through choosing to talk less and allowing myself the beauty of listening and making notes as I've gone along.

I'm a learner by nature and love to acquire new knowledge and then explore what it means and how it can be used. However, knowledge is only part of the process. What you do with it, and how you apply it, is where the differences become clear. Over and over and over again, I've been able to embrace a 'beginner' mindset, and that is why I keep learning. I've been able to share these ideas and concepts with others, playing with them in a messy way (where it's raw and vulnerable) and learning from them as we've gone along.

It's been enlightening and truly humbling to travel along so many paths over the last 10 years. The paths of so many brave and courageous people, from CEOs and senior leaders, to aspiring managers and entrepreneurs, plus the hundreds in between. I cannot thank them enough for allowing me that privilege.

How it works

Learning something new on your own can be daunting and scary. It doesn't always turn out as you expect, and you may get frustrated and give up part way through.

If you're someone who likes to research something beforehand, I've done the research for you over the last 10 years.

If you're someone that likes a plan and the reassurance of a solid road map, that's what this model will provide for you. If you're someone who doesn't like failing, then the model will empower you to do everything you possibly can to be successful. If you're someone that likes support and encouragement as you go along, each of the 6 Vs chapters is full of stories, exercises and questions to help you with that. Remember that there's also the option to sign up to 6 Steps to Achieving Your Vision of Success online programme. Just visit *Stucknowwhat.com* for details.

At each stage of the model, I'll be providing key takeaways and reflective questions at the end of each chapter. I've also devised some exercises to gently challenge and guide you along your journey. It is really important that you take the time to engage with these and complete them in your workbook as your answers will form your action plan for becoming unstuck. There is a natural flow, as I've set out within this book, so the process is much easier if you follow it in order.

Get your workbook here if you haven't already: stucknowwhat.com/resources

Start with vision and work through each part up to and including voice. Even where you're familiar with parts of the model, there is value in going over each area in the order it's been written. Your ideas may have changed, maybe as a result of just reading this book, and you may be able to dream bigger now.

You will find at the beginning of each chapter:

- An explanation of that particular V part of the model.

- Why it's important.

- The cost of not doing it.

- How to do the work in that part.

What this model can do for you

This process will:

1. Enable you to create a vision of where you want to be and a clear vision of success.

2. Help you to understand your own values.

3. Establish where you are now and what has to change.

4. Give you the tools you need to create a plan to make it happen.

5. Empower you to be able to execute your plan.

6. Equip you with the knowledge required to create your own support team (personal board members).

7. Change your view of fear and encourage you to boldly go after your dreams.

8. Transform your view of yourself and what you believe you're capable of achieving.

Making a difference

You're not alone in wanting to bring about change; many people are feeling:

- Unfulfilled at work.

- Dissatisfied with where they are in life.

- Like they can no longer motivate their team.

- Unhappy, and it has an effect on their mental health.

The Planning Manager who was plodding away

I took a call one evening from an existing client, asking me if I'd be able to help one of her close friends. Her friend was a little fed up and feeling pretty shit about work and life. She needed some help and thought she'd benefit from speaking to me. I suggested she put her friend in touch and said we'd go from there.

After a couple of days, I received a call. Instantly, through her tone, you could hear that she wasn't happy in her work or life. Her tone was gloomy, but still there was hope. Her energy was low, but it was not completely depleted.

I asked a few questions and just listened. After I set her an initial task, we agreed to meet in one week's time. Then we met again and she talked and I listened some more, before I replayed what I'd heard.

—"—

*Instead of choosing fear, I now
lead my life on the basis of what
could be possible.*

—"—

She wasn't happy and found herself plodding at work and generally stuck in her life. Her life was work, in the main. She didn't have a clear vision (or so she thought) and had no idea about her values. Her manager wasn't particularly helpful, but then he didn't really know how to help, only telling her that she needed to work on her confidence!

We worked together for the best part of a year. In that time, we covered all of the 6 Vs: vision, values, view, vehicle, valour and voice. The person who left at the end of our final session together was not the one who had been referred to me by her friend.

In her own words

'I remember coming home from work on countless days and always feeling like I was failing. Despite focusing all my efforts on my career, I always had a sense that I wasn't good enough. I was on the edge of losing my job, which to me would have been the end of the world. It culminated in coming home a nervous wreck after a particularly bad day and speaking to a close friend. She suggested I come and see you.

'Fast forward seven years. I've gone from Planning Assistant to Associate Director, running the planning service on my own. I hired a planning graduate and mentored him to become chartered. I led yoga classes, completed the three peaks challenge and two half-marathons. I got married and had a baby, before travelling around the world (literally) with our baby barely six months old.

'You were the catalyst in changing how I see the world. Instead of choosing fear, I now lead my life on the basis of what could be possible. I'm not sure I would have made such a fundamental change in how I see things if it wasn't for your mentoring.'

The international cricketer who was struggling

Back in 2013 I'd got to know an international physically disabled (PD) cricket team very well. My wife, Emma was their exercise scientist and she'd been working with the team for 18 months before she asked if I'd speak to one of the players. He was a middle order batsman, struggling with getting out early into his innings, leaving him in and out of the team as a result.

Not knowing what to expect, he rang me one day. We chatted for about 30 minutes about his season so far, about his good innings (and high scores) and his poor innings (a low or no score). When probed, he could tell me his vision and vision of success. He could also articulate some of his important values.

The parts that needed some work were:

- **Vehicle** – how you create an environment for change.

- **Victory** – ensuring success by identifying blockers.

- **Voice** – share your thoughts and build your support team.

Vehicle

Sport can be tough at times; there's pressure and expectation. Banter creeps into teams and it isn't always helpful, sometimes meaning that a dressing room can be a lonely place, as it was for him at times.

We looked at what he could do to influence this. We thought about how he could create some space, a moment for him to pause and gather his thoughts. He had a photograph someone had given him from a game where he scored a lot of runs and was enjoying himself. I got him to write down some words on the back of it and keep it in his kit bag. Before each innings, as he was padding up, he took it out and, because of that, he'd walk out onto the square with a different mindset.

Valour

One of his key blockers was his mindset and self-talk. He'd walk out onto the square telling himself (and believing) that he wasn't going to score many runs today, so minutes later he'd be back in the dressing room. We worked on what his self-talk could be, and I got him to practise it daily, ahead of the next game, the morning of the game and right up to walking out to bat. I also got him to share this with his partner, which I'll expand upon later.

Voice

There were a couple of people in the team who he was close to, people he could talk to about some of the work we'd been doing. His closest ally and supporter, however, was his partner (now wife); she was a huge encourager. I got him to share with her all the work we'd been doing, so she could act as a further reminder and give him a nudge at different times.

That summer he played pretty much every game for the team, and he made a contribution each time. His scores improved and he brought more to the team when they were fielding as well. In fact, he started to emerge as one of the leaders and voices within the dressing room.

Wherever you are right now, things can change. Small or large, change is absolutely possible, and often what's missing is just one part: a key to unlock the rest.

Key takeaways

- Having a vision of success provides you with focus.

- Knowing your values gets you moving forward.

- Where you are now is your catalyst (view).

- How you shape your environment becomes your vehicle.

- Seeing your obstacles as part of the way will empower you to show valour.

- Finding your voice will ensure you have the necessary support around you.

Questions to consider

1. What's on your 'life goal list' that you've been putting off?

2. Why are they not ticked off?

3. When would you have liked to have achieved some of those life goals by?

4. Who do you already have in your support team?

5. What if you had to start all over again, what would you do?

CREATING A VISION OF SUCCESS

*'The world is changed by your example,
not by your opinion.'*

PAULO COELHO

What is a Vision?

A vision tends to be something that is associated with organisations or with sporting teams. Search hard enough and you may find the vision on the corporate website as well; it's become a statement for why they exist.

But why can't you as an individual have one as well? After all, you have dreams and aspirations too.

—❝—

We can all be

dangerous dreamers.

—❞—

During my time at M&S Money the vision was:

'To be the first-choice provider of financial products for the Marks & Spencer shopper.'

There was a time when M&S had 10 million customers walking into their retail stores each week. If the business (M&S Money) could tap into a small percentage of those 10 million customers, then they wouldn't have to worry about trying to compete with other banks and financial institutions.

James Kerr, in his book, *Legacy*, talks about the New Zealand rugby team (the All Blacks).

He likes to quote Japanese proverbs and here's one that struck me:

'Vision without action is a dream.

Action without vision is a nightmare.'

Miles Hilton-Barber talks about being a 'dangerous dreamer' in his talks and on his audiobook, *Living Your Dreams*. There he takes the following from Lawrence of Arabia: 'All men dream, but not equally. Those who dream by night in the dusty recesses of their minds wake in the day to find that it was vanity, but the dreamers of the day are the dangerous dreamers, for they may act their dream with open eyes, that they may fulfil their dreams.'

We can all be dangerous dreamers.

So, I ask you again: why can't you as an individual have a vision too? The answer is, of course, that you not only can have a vision, you absolutely should have one. In this chapter, I'm going to show you how to create one using an exercise called 'vision of success'. I'll also show you how you can start to look at taking action.

Let me share a little more about what I mean in terms of a vision. As I explain when I'm working in organisations, teams or with individuals, a vision is aspirational. It's not about where you are now, though that is important, it's about where you want to be in the future, at a certain point. A point that is determined and set by you, and only you. This is what takes a vision and crafts it into a vision of success.

Your vision of success should be exciting and compelling for you. It should stir you inside and fire you up each morning. It doesn't matter what other people think about it because, guess what? They've got their own vision of success (or they should have), and it's different to yours.

What is the cost of not having your own Vision of success?

Take a moment. Think about the team, organisation or institution that you are part of currently. How many of the people alongside you have their own vision of success? Unless you're working for yourself (and even then, it can become blurred), very few people have a personal vision of success.

The reality is that those people who don't have a clear vision of success, ultimately subscribe to the vision of the team, organisation or institution that they are part of.

Does that ring true?

Consider this:

When you arrived at your current job, you would have gone through some type of induction. The vision and values were likely shared with you during this introduction stage. You may have received a talk from a senior director who reinforced them and reiterated the importance of you arriving at the company at that time. From the first day you were unconsciously signing up and subscribing to their vision of success.

Let me point out that there is nothing wrong with this at all. In part, it's how organisations, sporting teams and institutions grow and achieve success. A collective group of people, all working towards the same objective or cause (vision of success). Along the way, though, some of us get left behind. Why? Because our own ideas take a back seat. Not necessarily straight away, but certainly over time. We lose sight of what we're about and what's important to us, then we start to feel like we're losing control over our own destiny.

Think back to the manager waiting for retirement! Their vision of success had become retirement and everything that they associated with that. Perhaps it was being able to go on holidays, spend more time with the family or finally tick off things that had been on their bucket list for years.

The model for retirement is broken. For many of you reading this, the existing model for retirement simply won't be an option, so what other options do you have? We each have a choice. A choice to make now and in the years to come that will make them the best years of our lives, instead of waiting for something like retirement to happen (or not happen).

Rule 3 from the book *Taming Tigers* states: 'Head in the direction of where you want to arrive, every day.'

Let's look at how you can create your own vision of success.

How to create your Vision of success

Note: this is not about where you are today – it's about the future. The process below works best when you write your thoughts down. Fill in your answers for this exercise and all others in the free Stuck workbook which you should have by now! This is where you should fill in all the answers to these exercises. If you haven't printed it out already you can download it here: stucknowwhat.com/resources. This allows you to get things out of your head, so it's important not to critique yourself; just go with your instinct and don't judge.

VISION EXERCISE:

Planning where you want to be

Step 1: Dream

Allow yourself to dream and be creative.

1. Where do you want to be in the future? (Same company, doing something different or somewhere else?)

2. What do you want to be doing in the future? (Different role or different industry?)

3. At what point in the future? (Six months, one year, five years etc.?)

It's up to you to decide the timescale. It can be short, medium or long term. Avoid falling into the corporate trap of asking: in two years' time where do you want to be? Two years might not be soon enough for you! Alternatively, you may be working towards a longer-term vision of success.

Step 2: Start a plan

Allow yourself to consider what else needs to happen to facilitate Step 1.

What will you **not** be doing at this point in the future? (Something to be delegated to others or that is not required of you in the future.)

Who will be with you? (Taking on additional responsibilities or supporting you.)

Step 3: Way forward

Allow yourself to explore next steps following Step 2.

1. What one thing can you do first of all? (Now, almost instantly.)

2. What other actions can you expect to take in the next two weeks? (Capture ideas at this point.)

Now, you have the basis of your vision of success. You know where you want to be (and when) and the types of things you want to be doing. You also know what you don't want to be doing and some of the actions you can start to take.

It will start to take more shape as you:

- Sit with it and ponder more.

- Walk away and come back to it.

- Adapt and tweak parts.

- Share it with others.

- Ask yourself if this is what you truly want.

The Sales Manager who wanted to become a Director

In June 2018, I was invited into a digital marketing company to do some work with the senior manager group. The company had built up a good reputation and established itself as a leading partner for Google. They were looking to grow over the next two to five years and saw the senior management group playing a big part in the company's growth.

One of the first sessions that I ran with the senior managers was called 'You and your leadership'. There were three main focus areas within the day:

1. You as a leader (leadership proposition)

2. Your vision of success and values

3. Building trust

It was during the 'vision of success' exercise that I started to get some challenges and push back from some within the group. Clearly this wasn't an exercise they'd done before, or if they had, they'd not shared the results amongst their peers and colleagues.

One of the more, shall we say, outspoken managers was happy to share his vision of success with the rest of the group. I was later told by the group that this was no surprise. However, at that stage I was still getting to know the managers, individually and collectively.

He confidently shared with his colleagues and myself, that his vision of success was to become the Sales Director within two years. At this point he was the Sales Manager. I liked the fact that he'd been bold enough in sharing first. He'd shown that he was open to being vulnerable amongst his peers. This was something that I referenced a number of times to the group, the leadership team and subsequent groups that I have worked with.

Whilst he still had some work to do in terms of shaping his vision of success and gaining clarity on the steps (and actions) that he would need to take, he'd made a great start.

With that start, his first effort, if you like, the passion and hunger to succeed were obvious to those around him. The intent was clear to himself and to others. The values exercise that followed highlighted the key drivers that would enable and empower him towards achieving his vision of success.

I believe that it doesn't take much to keep people engaged and motivated in the workplace. You do, though, have to spend a little bit of time with them, helping them and you to understand their 'vision of success' and values.

In terms of the Sales Manager, he's now the Head of Sales. He has a Sales Manager and another manager working alongside him. He is continuing on his path towards becoming a Sales Director, whilst others, who perhaps weren't as clear with their vision of success or as bold with their execution, continue to do the same role today as they did then.

<u>Note:</u> if you're happy in your current role but would like to bring about some changes, having a clear vision of success will help provide you with clarity about what you can do next. It's not exclusive to your next career move.

The part-time bank collector who dared to dream

Back in 2010, I was doing some coaching and training with business owners in the northwest of England. One of the business owners ran a networking company. Their business brought together other business owners in the local area, for training events as well as providing a members' discount programme.

I met a woman at one particular event who was, at the time, working part-time in the collections department of a renowned high street bank. I quickly learned that she'd provided the cakes as part of the morning's refreshments, but that wasn't all I discovered.

To say she didn't enjoy her job would be an understatement; it sucked the life out of her, leaving her dreading going into work. Her only saving grace was that she worked part-time hours. It was her way of contributing to the household.

I complimented her on the cakes and said she had a real talent. Modestly, she shared that she loved baking and made cakes for family and friends. It was just a hobby, she said, but I could tell it was more than that. Her face lit up and she became animated when sharing stories of some of the cakes she'd made in the last couple of months.

'How does it compare to your day job?' I asked.

'It doesn't,' was her answer. And then she proceeded to talk about her job, without the energy or enthusiasm I'd witnessed only minutes before.

What if you could bake cakes for a living? What would you need to do? These questions were met with the expected (and typical) resistances and excuses. At this point, she hadn't thought about it or considered what a different vision of success might look like.

I continued and asked her how many cupcakes she would need to sell each week to make the same amount of money as she did working for the bank. This got her thinking, but she didn't know the answer. I didn't expect her to either at that point.

The conversation continued to focus on baking as she shared more stories about people that she'd already sold cakes to; baking was definitely more than a hobby, and clearly work had not been working for her for some time. It was great to witness the energy and passion she had for cooking.

As I left the networking event, I caught up with her on the way out. She was smiling as others had also complimented her on her cakes. I encouraged her to work out the numbers and offered to meet up with her if she wanted some help and support.

By the time we spoke a couple of weeks later, she'd worked out some numbers. More importantly, she'd allowed herself some time and space to think. She'd spoken with her husband, who was a builder, and she had the start of a vision of success, and it would involve using the home kitchen to begin with.

It was exciting and energising for her, but it was also scary and there was a lot to do. However, the high street bank was not part of it! Her energy and enthusiasm to get started blew me away.

Within three months she'd left her job at the bank to pursue her vision of success. Her vision would become a reality; she started at home, initially, before moving to the same premises where we had first met at the networking event.

Sadly, that building burned down. However, new premises were acquired, and the business continued to grow. Her sister joined the business, and they built a reputation for themselves in Chester and the surrounding areas.

<u>Note:</u> once you've achieved one vision of success, the likelihood is you'll start thinking (at some point) about the next one. Your vision of success will change as you go through life and bring about change. The bank collector who set up a cake business has built on her initial success and now manages a portfolio of properties.

Personal reflection

OK, it's a lot to take in. I get that – it was for me too. Stepping away from the comfort of what you know takes courage. Some of you won't ever have had or indeed thought about a vision of success, and yet you've done OK or alright, or so you tell yourself. You may have moved around or bounced from job to job, without really giving your career much thought.

Well, that was me as well. Five years in hospitality, with university sandwiched in the middle of it, followed by 10 years in retail and the financial services. I never really had a clear vision of success; I simply went after the next job up from mine. When that wasn't available, something tended to present itself as an alternative option. This approach served me well, up to a point.

That point was when I realised (or thought) that my time on this planet was limited. That feeling in my stomach was indescribable, but it changed everything. Like the person whose test results come back with the dreaded bad news, everything else seemed less important and was put on hold. Quickly life became about living.

Many of you will wait and sit things out. Close friends or colleagues will comfort you and tell you everything will be OK or tomorrow is another day. This is until the pain that you're experiencing (in whatever area of your life) becomes too much. Only then does it cause you to rethink an element of your life and make a change. But it doesn't have to be this way, for you, me or anyone; there are always other options.

Like I've said, though, many of you have never had or considered creating a clear vision of success for yourself. Why should you when it's not taught through education or encouraged and passed on by previous generations?

It's scary, yes, but never as scary as we tell ourselves in our own mind. Allow yourself to be a 'dangerous dreamer' like Miles Hilton-Barber. After all, he only began living his dreams from the age of 50!

— Key takeaways ——————

- Create your own vision of success by following my three steps (dream, plan, way forward).

- Your vision of success doesn't have to be your next career move, it can be just as effective when looking at your next challenge or objective.

- Share your vision of success with others because it makes it feel real.

- Start by taking the first few actions towards achieving your vision of success and you will build momentum.

— Questions to consider——————

1. What could your vision of success be?

2. Why is it important to you?

3. Who could you share it with initially?

4. Who else could help you shape it?

5. What if you achieved your vision of success? What would it allow you to do?

6. Do external things distract you?

'Then make time for yourself to learn something worthwhile; stop letting yourself be pulled in all directions. But make sure you guard against the other kind of confusion. People who labour all their lives but have no purpose to direct every thought and impulse toward are wasting their time – even when hard at work.'

MARCUS AURELIUS – MEDITATIONS BOOK 2.7

An empowering piece of writing from Marcus Aurelius; your vision of success becomes your purpose, so it starts and ends with you. You have the power within you already to bring about change.

CHAPTER 8

THE VALUE OF KNOWING YOUR VALUES

'Values are like fingerprints. Nobody's are the same, but you leave them all over everything you do.'

ELVIS PRESLEY

What are Values?

Like a vision, values tend to be something that are associated with organisations or with sporting teams. Sometimes they can be found on the wall in reception or the entrance of an organisation. Between you and me,

—❝—

When you become aware
of your values, it changes
everything.

—❞—

and I've seen this in at least two organisations that I worked for, values are sometimes even stuck on the back of toilet doors!

'Why?' you might ask. Well, you'd have to ask the leadership or HR team to find out the real reason. I suspect it's because people tend to spend a significant amount of time in the loo and, in many cases, organisations are desperately trying to make values 'stick'. If you search hard enough, you may find the values on the corporate website as well.

They are not just reminders for existing employees but also statements to attract potential new recruits or new customers. Generally, they provide a little bit of insight into how the company or team operates.

In this chapter, I'm going to help you to understand more about your own values and show you how to find out which values are most important to you. Why? Because values are more than just a set of words. There is meaning attached to each of your values, which you may or may not realise at the moment, and this meaning translates into your daily behaviours in all aspects of your life.

When you become aware of your values, it changes everything. Carry on with your discovery and I'll explain how you can take positive action when your important values aren't aligned or present in your current job.

Why are Values important?

Firstly, let me share a little more about what I mean in terms of values.

> *'When your values are clear to you, making decisions becomes easier.'*

ROY E DISNEY

The way that I explain values to teams and individuals is that they are: *why you do what you do, in the way that you do it.*

From the outside it looks like you are just going about your daily business. For you, it may just be the same, as you may never have considered what your values are before, but it goes deeper than that. Your values show up when you're at your happiest and also when you're at your unhappiest.

How so?

Unconsciously, you've been programmed from an early age: the good, the bad and the indifferent. Remember the 'computer brain' explained in Chapter 4? That is where your values are stored. Using another popular illustration, imagine an iceberg for a moment. What you see above the surface of the water is only a small amount of the iceberg. In human terms, above the surface is where you can see your results and behaviours. Underneath is where your values are, alongside your beliefs, motivations, assumptions and biases. When you've done the values exercise in this chapter, ask yourself – how are your values driving your behaviours and ultimately your results right now? It's (scarily in some cases) obvious!

Here's the thing (I'm generalising again): most people have no idea about their values and the importance of them. Knowing them personally, changes everything for you.

What is the cost of not identifying your personal Values?

Being aware of people's values from an organisational point of view will save a company thousands in pay rises each year! From a team perspective, your chances of success also increase considerably.

Why don't organisations, institutions and sports teams find out what values are important to individuals? Simply put, it takes time and effort. In the majority of cases, they're caught up in being busy, focused on their own vision and values or strategy, or doing what they've always done, but they're missing a trick! They're also missing out on making a positive contribution to other areas of the business, including: employee engagement, retention, wellbeing and loyalty.

The cost to you

The personal cost of not identifying and understanding your own values is what I see in every organisation or team I spend time with; apathy and disgruntlement is rife, leaving large portions of the workforce demotivated.

Think back to the stories of the manager waiting for retirement or the Diet Coke manager. Both had a clear idea of what they did and didn't want in their lives at those particular points in time.

I don't know their values for sure, as I've not done a values exercise with either person. However, in the instance of the manager waiting for retirement, she's likely to have had the personal value of security in her top five values, alongside recognition and accountability. She had been given different roles and responsibilities during my last few years in the business and was recognised by her peers. A value of security can keep someone in an organisation, as they're unlikely to walk away (as I did) or take significant risks.

Going back to the Diet Coke manager, she's likely to have had a personal value of adventure in her top five values, perhaps alongside travel and helping others. She was fed up and had been for some time; working in a builder's merchant wasn't enabling her to see the world and travel, but teaching English as a foreign language would (and did).

The cost of not discovering your personal values are, at best:

- You sort of fit into an organisation and how they operate.

- You carry on with what you're doing, occasionally getting frustrated.

- You get overlooked at times and wonder why you bother.

At worst:

- You struggle in terms of identity and finding where you're at your best.

- You battle through days and move from job to job, never really being satisfied.

- You moan to your loved ones at home and take your frustration out on them.

You have a choice to make; go with what you know or choose a new path of discovery. It's simple really. What will you decide to do?

How to discover your own personal Values

This is one of my favourite exercises to do with people. Why? Because it never ceases to amaze me what comes out of it in terms of insight and realisation. You can't ignore what's on the paper when you see it in front of you.

VALUES EXERCISE:

Establishing what's really important

First, you'll need the worksheet that can be found in the free Stuck workbook. If you haven't download yours at stucknowwhat.com/resources

Step 1: In the context of...

You can change this context from work to relationships to health to love. For now, though, let's look at work. You're looking for short one or two word answers. Write each new answer on a separate line.

1. In the context of work, what's important to you? (Note these down.)

2. What else? (And add.)

3. What else? (And add.)

4. What else? (And so on until you start to repeat what you've written already.)

5. Draw a line under your last answer.

Step 2: A time when you were motivated

Can you think of a time in your career when you were motivated? What were you doing? (Make a mental note.) Now, continue to add the following answers to your piece of paper underneath your previous answers.

1. What was motivating about it?

2. And what else?

3. What did it allow you to do?

4. And what else?

5. Once you start to repeat your answers or answers from Step 1, stop and draw a line under your last answer.

Step 3a: Would cause you to leave

Pause and reflect on your list of values so far, then write down the following answers:

Hypothetically, if all those values were present in your job right now:

1. What would cause you to leave?

2. What else? (And add.)

3. What else? (And add.)

4. Once you start repeating answers, draw a line under your last one.

Step 3b: Would cause you to stay!

Allow yourself some time to reflect on your list of values so far before writing your answer to the following:

Hypothetically, if all those values were present in your job right now:

1. What else would cause you to stay?

2. Once you start repeating answers, draw a line under your last one.

Step 4: Rewrite your list

Look at all of the work values you've written down.

1. Rewrite your list in priority 1–20 (or however many you have written down).

2. Aim to do this in 60–90 seconds.

Let's see what's most important to you.

3. Write out on a separate piece of paper your top five values.

4. Tick or highlight the values that are currently being

met in your job today.

5. Note that there are no half measures with values. You can't have half a tick. It's either happening or not right now.

Step 5: Reveal

Here's where the insight and reality check happen.

1. What do your results tell you?

If you've got four or five of your (top five) values present, then you're likely to be happy where you are right now. You're likely to have positive energy about your work and the impact you're having.

If you've got three of your values present, then you're likely to be experiencing some frustration with the work you're doing, or with the people you work with. If left (unaddressed) this can cause a negative impact on some of your other important values.

If you've got one or two values present, then you're likely to be frustrated or pissed off with work right now. There's a good chance you're moaning to others about it and you're likely to be updating your CV and LinkedIn profile (if you haven't done so already).

If none of your values are present, then there's a good chance that mentally you've left your job and company already. Similar to having one or two values present, you're likely to be pissed off and frustrated with what you're doing. What you may not realise is that your productivity and attendance will start to drop (if it hasn't already). You're also going to start to have a negative impact on those around you (if that hasn't started to happen already).

The leader whose personal Values weren't being met

Back in 2015, I enrolled to do a Level 7 coaching and mentoring qualification through the Institute of Leadership & Management, to further enhance my coaching knowledge and experience to date. Part of the programme, as you'd expect, included a substantial amount of one-to-one and group coaching.

I reached out to my network to see if any of them would like to receive some free coaching. Another coach, whom I'd got to know very well, suggested someone she knew who was working in the third sector. This immediately got me interested because I'd not worked in this area previously.

An email exchange and one telephone call later, and I was working with a leader for an organisation tackling poverty and homelessness in Manchester and the surrounding areas. We'd built up a bit of rapport and I arrived in Manchester on a rainy morning, excited and looking forward to getting started.

The first session tends to involve an element of discovery with the other person, getting a feel for their background and exploring what their vision of success is. He'd been involved in the third sector, working with volunteers, for a number of years. He was drawn to this sector and felt this was where he could make the biggest difference. Outside of working for his current employer, he shared that he also did some private one-to-one coaching.

Working with a fellow coach is intriguing and insightful. Whilst your primary role is to coach, you get to experience the additional joy of learning yourself, but this isn't always the case. I met a coach earlier in my career who avoided me and saw me as a threat to her coaching practice!

Anyway, the omens were good in this case and we quickly established a clear vision of success and a timeline for us to work together. What I was more intrigued about (as I always am) was understanding his values. What did he hold dear to himself that would either drive him towards success or hold him back? It didn't take long to understand what his values were and what was important to him.

With a little encouragement, he reeled off his top five values in order. They were:

1. Creativity

2. Physical activity and health

3. Family and friends

4. Working with people (transforming lives and society)

5. Space for reflection (spirituality and self-development)

Leaders (and other people) with good self-awareness and emotional intelligence tend to be able to share their values with little or no thought. In this case, these had become ingrained. The interesting part was understanding which values were being met at that particular moment in time.

He'd taken an extra step and rated each of his top five values out of 10. A score of less than 5 suggests a value is rarely being met. A score of 5 to 7 suggests that a value is being met sometimes. A score above 7 suggests that a value is being frequently met.

1. Creativity - 5

2. Physical activity and health - 5

3. Family and friends - 5

4. Working with people (transforming lives and society) - 6

5. Space for reflection (spirituality and self-development) - 7

When you look at the results above, it's difficult not to jump to your own conclusions. It's human nature to do so, but a good coach won't. They know the importance and value in getting the person to draw their own conclusions.

On the face of it, only two out of his top five values were some way to being met. In this instance, he'd already drawn his conclusions and realised that things needed to change. He shared with me that he'd started thinking about how he could address those values that weren't being met. He'd spoken with his wife and close friends about work and the impact he felt it was having on his motivation and energy. This is more common than you think, and the conversations that you have with your partner or friends after work are usually a good indicator as to whether your important values are being met or not.

To be fair to this guy, he'd already begun making some changes. It was a case that would be an easy fix, if he'd known how to understand and discover his values. If you manage and lead people, this will serve you better than any incentive. It will also ensure every performance review or appraisal is worthwhile.

Personal reflection

Right now, I don't know what's happening in your life. I don't know your circumstances or career path to date. I do, however, have a pretty good idea that your thoughts are starting to make links and associations back and forth between work and conversations you've been having with the important people in your life. Your partner, your parents, your friends. Oh yes, I bet they've been on the receiving end of many a download.

You see, as much as you try to put a positive spin on things, those conversations will invariably have been negative ones. They will have focused on the things you're not happy about or the things that are pissing you off.

If work is working for you, then great. The likelihood is in that instance that your values are being met. If it's not working for you, which is the case for many people, then values are a bloody good place to start in terms of seeing answers on a piece of paper and starting to work out a way forward. I know this to be true because I've witnessed it over and over and over again, especially in the corporate world.

Now, I personally believe: *It doesn't take a lot to keep people happy – you just need to be able to understand their values.* When you do that, leading and managing people becomes easy; employee engagement scores go up and absence rates go down.

Organisations that get caught up with their own vision and values often end up neglecting the very people who play the biggest part in delivering them. There's never been a better time for organisations to take their people through the values exercise so they can understand their personal values. I've seen first-hand a shift in personal values, having revisited values with several clients during the coronavirus pandemic.

What was important to some people at the start of 2020 changed significantly as people adapted to working from home. My advice to any employer is: if you only do one thing with your employees as they transition back into the office or move to a more flexible working arrangement, then definitely invest some time to understand their values.

Each of us has our own personal values. In fact, my own personal values came into conflict with an organisation's values and way of operating back in 2011 when I worked for a mobile phone retailer. It is the only job I've ever taken based on money. I needed a job and I had responsibilities towards my children. Within three months of taking that job, I'd resigned.

Why? My personal values were being challenged and compromised. It was a hard decision because I had responsibilities. It was an easy decision because my important personal values were not being met and it was causing me stress, anxiety and some anger.

One of my values is family and being told that working at the mobile phone retailer was a lifestyle choice, and not a career, didn't sit well with me. Being told that if they needed me in work at the weekend to design training material then I was expected to be in work wasn't going to work. So, I fronted up and had the conversations with my line manager and director.

Fortunately for me, I had a manager who was both understanding and supportive. She recognised the skills and experience that I brought to the Learning and Development (L&D) team and to the business. Because of her, I was offered the opportunity to be interviewed for another role within L&D, in the management development team. Working alongside my new manager, I flourished. Without their understanding of my values, several of the stories in this book would not have been possible.

— Key takeaways ———————————

- Remember that your values are personal to you and usually different to those of others.

- Work out what your personal values are and discover if they are a good fit with what you're doing currently.

- Share your values with others and they will start to understand a) what gets you out of bed in the morning and b) why you do what you do, in the way that you do it.

- Be bold enough to take action if your top five values are no longer being met.

- It's your responsibility to bring about change.

— Questions to consider ———————————

1. What values do you value most in your work?

2. Why are these values important to you?

3. How are these values serving you (or not) currently?

4. Who have you shared them with? Who can you?

5. What would be better values for you if, currently, some are not serving you well?

CHAPTER 9

YOUR VIEW: RIGHT HERE, RIGHT NOW

'Logic defeats anger, because anger even when it's justified can quickly become irrational. So, use cold hard logic on yourself.'

EPICTETUS

What is your current View?

The biggest obstacle preventing you from moving towards your vision of success is your current reality. Your current reality is your current view. How do I know this? Well, the truth is that you've allowed yourself to get comfortable in your current role and your current surroundings. Perhaps you got that promotion or pay rise.

Maybe you achieved all of your targets or got to attend that external development programme. Or you may simply have had your annual appraisal recently and the future is looking good for you, if you just achieve 'x' and 'y' in this coming year.

All of these things should sound familiar to you; organisations have been using these tools and incentives for decades as a way of retaining you, without them doing the hard work. I know because I got a pay increase pretty much every year during my time at M&S Money.

The hard work is finding out what your vision of success is, and what values are important to you. Now, would you agree that where you are today is not where you want to be in the future? Good. Do you want to be a dreamer at night, but one who wakes in the morning and forgets? Or are you ready to do the work to make the changes happen?

Remember, the easiest thing you can do is to carry on doing what you're already doing. Simply cast your mind back to the opening chapter and you have:

- A boring routine.

- A grind.

- A feeling of being stuck and on a treadmill.

A change requires effort and energy and that's why it's important to use cold, hard logic on yourself in this next phase. In this chapter, I'm going to help you to get really

Cold hard facts have no time for excuses.

clear on your current view so that you are able to understand what you need to be focusing on in order to bring
about change. I'll also explain how you can build on what's
currently working for you and use this to your advantage
in the future.

Why is being clear on your View so important?

The cold, hard facts of your current situation and view are
crucial. Stripped of emotion and attachment, this may seem
harsh, but it's meant to be harsh – that's the point. Why?
Because you've got really good at kidding yourself. You've
been telling yourself that you want to do the work, but
sometimes it's hard and so you start to make excuses.

In many cases, you will have developed networks across
social media that feed your ego and reassure you when you
make excuses. That day when you didn't achieve a great
deal and so wrote it off. You chose to share it across social
media and hear others say that it's OK, and that we all have
days like that.

In the context of you and bringing about change; is this
helpful? Not at all, but the ego feels better! Once you make
excuses, your ego has won. Very quickly you can begin to
pat yourself on the back for what you have done, rather
than being hard on yourself for what you haven't done.

Cold hard facts have no time for excuses. They simply present to you how the situation is. When you can see them,

preferably written down in front of you, you have a choice: do something with them or continue to make excuses. I too, was guilty of making excuses earlier in my career. Until I took personal responsibility and started to change my view.

In the words of Alfred, Lord Tennyson: 'It is better to have tried and failed than to live life wondering what would have happened if I'd tried.' Let these words act as a reminder to you as you seek clarity within your current view.

What is the cost of not identifying your current View?

It's a choice that you're making – it's the choice to carry on doing the same thing with little or nothing changing. You're choosing **not** to explore what might be. This is what happens when you don't identify and evaluate where you are currently. You can even go so far as convincing yourself that actually things are OK or better than they really are.

Ultimately, you accept your current situation and circumstances. You deem your own values not important enough to change and so begin to accept the values of others. If this is you right now, then you are staying stuck because you've resigned yourself to more of the daily grind. Without knowing it, you're choosing to prioritise this state over your personal health and wellbeing. If you're already overworking too, then this will undoubtedly lead to stress in your life. As outlined in Chapter 2, that stress can develop into anxiety for some people, which in turn can lead to feeling depressed or burnt out. This is the cost of not doing something about your current view today in relation to your values and vision of success.

Remember the quick test in Chapter 1? Are you caught up in the daily grind? How many of those questions did you answer 'yes' to?

How to get clarity on your current View

The most effective way to get clarity on your current view is to cast your mind back to your values and (vision) vision of success. It's likely that you have started to get some clarity about your vision of success at this stage and what your important values are. So where are the gaps?

VIEW EXERCISE:

Identifying what's working and what needs changing

Grab the worksheet from the free Stuck workbook and fill in your answers to the following.

Step 1: In terms of your Vision

1. What are you currently doing that can help and enable you to move positively towards your goal?

For example, let's look again at the Sales Manager in Chapter 7. He was a good motivator, achieving results through his team, and good at influencing the leadership team.

Similarly, this could be you if you're looking at your next promotion. Things that you're good at that might help you are:

- Being a good communicator.

- Planning and organising.

- Having the ability to get buy-in from others with new ideas or initiatives.

2. What are you **not** doing currently that, if you were to start, you could begin to move towards achieving your vision of success?

Again, it's clear if I use the same example of the Sales Manager. He acknowledged that he needed to delegate more to his team, empower others to take on responsibility and look to take on more strategic responsibilities himself.

Looking at yourself once more, if you are like him, you may need to develop in areas such as:

- Influencing upwards.

- Delivering presentations to groups.

- Understanding talent development and progression.

Step 2: In terms of your Values

1. Which of your values (that are currently being met or are in place) can help drive you towards your vision of success?

For example, let's look at the leader in Chapter 8. His values of 'working with people (transforming lives and society) and personal space for reflection' were at the time being met or partly met. This enabled him to create space for reflection naturally. It also ensured that his value of 'working with people' could be directly linked to his vision of success and transforming lives.

2. Which of your values are not currently being met but can be worked on or changed to enable you to move forward positively?

Again, using the same example as above; his values of 'creativity, physical activity and health, friends and family' were being neglected or only met in part. He had been consciously aware of this for some time. His challenge (as he put it to me) was to find ways to get a better balance back in these areas as they positively contributed towards his vision of success. Indeed, when he was exercising more regularly, he naturally felt more creative.

When you choose to approach change in this way, there's intention involved. Focusing on your vision of success and values gets your mind in a positive state – a state of excitement and curiosity about what might be and what is coming next. This positive mindset (or growth mindset) is what allows each of us to grow and continue to develop. Ultimately, this is what you need to leverage and build upon.

The leader who was questioning their Vision and Values

Towards the end of 2019, I was listening to a friend's podcast and his guest on that particular show was talking about vulnerability and goals. She was (and still is) a director of a company in the US that focuses on end-of-life services. She's been there for 20 years.

What struck me as I listened to her speak was a disconnect between what she was doing and what she wanted to do. When I scratched under the surface a little, I found that she'd written herself a letter and published this on her personal website. Here's a short extract from that letter:

'The overriding emotion for the year will be that of "treading water" and feeling lost. Treading water is like employing energy without getting anywhere. You are accustomed to doing and seeing results. What is this bit about spending energy (and lots of it) to get nowhere? This will also drive you to ACT and take action.'

There it is on the page, an acknowledgement of a disconnect. This is the reality for all to see and bear witness to; a person whose current role is no longer matching her vision of success or values.

Kirsty Mac says: 'You meet yourself on the page.'

What followed was an exchange of messages that then culminated in us having a Zoom conversation in January 2020. During that conversation it was obvious that something wasn't quite right. There were moments when I could sense her passionate energy, genuine zest for life and love of helping others. Equally, though, I could feel a sense of frustration coming from her.

Our initial conversation was brief, but we continued to exchange more messages in the following weeks. It's worth noting that nothing had changed up to this point. Then one day something did happen. I had been doing some work on values with a corporate client, as part of their management programme, and it was fresh in my mind.

Out of curiosity, I asked her if she knew what her important values were or if she'd ever done a values exercise. No, was her response. I explained a little bit about values to her. I just covered the little things, like how they drive us and the importance they play each day. I could feel that energy and passion coming back down the line and we arranged another Zoom call to go through her values.

We had the Zoom call as planned, and I took her through the values exercise outlined in Chapter 8. Having elicited a number of values during this exercise, approximately 18–20 in total, I asked her to write them out in order of priority before writing out separately her top five.

Watching her do this was hugely insightful. A smile or a slight shift of the head were visibly noticeable as she stopped and paused at each of her values. You could see that she was in tune with what her important values were. The process of prioritising happened instinctively and quickly. It often does.

The unaware or untrained eye can easily miss these things. For her, like me observing, there were subtle reinforcements or acknowledgments in her mind. There was a confirmation of certain thoughts that she'd been having (perhaps recently) about what was and wasn't feeling right or in sync in her life.

You can't underestimate the power of seeing this exercise unfold before your eyes. It's a huge realisation for the individual (as it was in this case as well) and, for me, it's a huge privilege to be able to witness it. Like the letter she'd written to herself, the words on the page were confirmation once more of a disconnect and something not being right.

Her top five values were:

1. Being seen and valued

2. Creativity (being inventive with scarce resources)

3. Empowering others to move forward

4. Engaging and connecting with others

5. Learning and development

The main observations were:

1. Her number one value of being seen and valued was not being met.

2. Whilst there were opportunities to be creative in her role, these weren't always valued by others.

3. She's naturally a people person and looks to empowers others.

4. The other two values were being met.

The key here is that her top two values weren't being met or satisfied. Consequently, she has been actively pursuing values 4 and 5 over the last 18 months (at least). Together with her third value being met, she's remained in her current role and employment (for now).

When we explored what her vision of success was, she didn't have a clear one. She was feeling stuck between where she was and what she was doing versus where she would like to be – which is a place that's better aligned with her values.

Currently, she's doing the work to gain clarity on her vision of success whilst looking closely at her personal values. This could just as easily be you right now, and it is more common than you might think. Ask yourself what was your last annual appraisal or performance review like? Did it excite you and leave you feeling empowered for the next 12 months? Or has it got you thinking, 'I can't be doing this in 12 months' time'?

Personal reflection

I see so many people get to this point on the journey and then just freeze. They've started the work of creating their vision of success and, as a result, they've found a new level of energy in their life. It's exciting and exhilarating in many cases; it's a way out and/or a way forward.

Here's the thing, though. People freeze because the gap between where they are now and where they want to be appears to be too big. Some people would rather choose the unhappiness (of where they are right now) over any uncertainty along the journey towards their vision of success.

The freeze literally causes them to hesitate or pull back. They retreat, in some cases, to the comfortableness of what they know. Even though they know, in their heart of hearts, that it's not going to help them.

If your vision of success is 18–24 months or more in the future, then your motivation, drive and focus will be questionable. All of us are bombarded everyday with the quick fix, life hack, achieve-it-now messaging that marketers know will distract and captivate our imaginations instantly. As discussed in the opening chapters, this book and the approaches within it are based around taking back control over the work you do and bringing about changes in your life.

In the case of myself, you could say that I've been 'working on' writing this book since March 2016! In that time, I've sat and reflected on my 'current view' many times and not done anything about it! When I look back to my journal entry on 2nd March 2016, I'm reminded of two important pieces of wisdom I wrote down:

1. *'We are writing the story of our lives.'*
   Jim Lawless, *Taming Tigers*

2. **Alice:** *Would you tell me, please, which way I ought to go from here?*

   The Cheshire Cat: *That depends a good deal on where you want to get to.*

   Alice: *I don't much care where.*

   The Cheshire Cat: *Then it doesn't much matter which way you go.*

   Alice: *... So long as I get somewhere.*

   The Cheshire Cat: *Oh, you're sure to do that, if only you walk long enough.*

   Lewis Carroll, *Alice's Adventures in Wonderland*

These two pieces of wisdom have remained with me throughout the last four years. You could say that the hard work for me began once I left my publisher's office in London on 16th March 2020 and headed back home to the northwest of England instead of travelling on to Winchester to facilitate two days with one of my clients.

The key decisions that I took before that day, though, ultimately kickstarted my journey towards becoming a published author. I told myself that if I was going to move from my current view to achieving my vision of success, then

I needed to start making some different decisions. Those decisions towards the end of 2019 included:

- Saying 'no' to some of the work that I'd previously done with other training organisations.

- Relinquishing my licence to host DisruptHR Edinburgh.

- Putting back or on hold other project collaborations.

- Pausing my podcast after series four.

Then in January/February 2020 I discovered Known Publishing and, after a couple of conversations, struck up a great rapport with Ali and Leila.

A reminder to everyone who gets to this stage and starts to freeze: 'Nothing changes, if nothing changes.' Your current view isn't your only view. What you see on the page before you is your starting point. The opportunity is what lies ahead.

— Key takeaways —

- Wherever you are right now, change can happen as long as you're clear on your vision of success and values.

- You don't have to wait for your next performance review or appraisal before making changes to your situation.

- What is pissing you off now is also likely to be pissing you off in 12 months, unless you take action.

- Cold hard facts trump emotion and excuses every time.

— Questions to consider —

1. What's not being met from a values perspective that you can change or influence in the next 30 days?

2. Why have you allowed yourself to get stuck in your current situation?

3. Who haven't you shared this with?

4. Who can help you to address your current situation?

5. What if you were doing a role in your current workplace that was linked to your vision of success and values, what would it look like?

CHAPTER 10

YOUR VEHICLE ───
FOR CHANGE

'If you wait for opportunities to occur,
you will be one of the crowd.'

EDWARD DE BONO

What is the Vehicle?

By design and definition, a vehicle is a mode of transport and something that moves. Put simply, this is how you get from A to B. In this case, it's how you move from your current view to arriving at your vision of success. Only it's not necessarily simple – if it was, everyone would be doing it, and they're not!

This stage is all about creating an environment that becomes your vehicle for change. You're building on the work that you've already done in identifying your vision and vision of success. You're building on the foundation of your values. Note that this is **not** about putting together any old plan. Instead, this is about:

1. Understanding and being clear on what your current circumstances and environment are.

Once you've done that, then it's about:

2. How you create an actionable plan that is going to work for you.

You need a plan that both excites you and drives you every single day. If it doesn't do both of these things, then you've not got the right plan. Your plan should be challenging yet achievable in relation to your current circumstances. This chapter is all about setting you up for maximum success and limiting failure where possible.

Take note, though: this is the stage where people often fall down or give up. Not intentionally, but it does happen.

Imagine you've created your perfect vision, but you never reach it – how sad would that be? Anyone can get fired up and energised by their vision and by picturing their success. You can talk about this and that and how things are going to be different, but you can't overlook the two most important things in this process: accountability and action.

Unrealistic plans quickly lead to inaction and feelings of being overwhelmed.

Putting things off or trying to do it all on your own has a similar effect. I'll share more around the importance of accountability and having a coach or buddy to support you in Chapter 11.

As my good friend Dig says, 'you never get this time back, so make the most of it now'.

One of the joys of working with a coach is that they'll help you to take action. I love helping people do this. For now, though, hold those two words in mind: accountability and action. The challenge for you with your vehicle is to create a plan that excites and drives you as much as your vision and vision of success.

Why is creating a Vehicle for change so important?

As I've mentioned in the 6 V Model chapters so far, a number of changes are required if you are to arrive at the point of achieving your vision of success. You are very unlikely to achieve this by relying on what you already know or have done in the past; what's got you to this point, won't necessarily get you to the next point. And the same is true of your current environment. You don't need to be reminded of Einstein's quote to realise this; if you rely on what you've done before, it's likely that you'll get more of the same or fall short.

— **"** —

If you rely on what you've done before, it's likely that you'll get more of the same or fall short.

— **"** —

Missed opportunities

I worked at M&S Money for nearly 10 years. During that time, 7 out of 10 of my annual appraisals had one thing in common: my number one development area was planning and organising. This was especially true of my time working in L&D. Every manager I had praised me for my work over the previous 12 months and then said those dreaded words...

If only you worked on your planning skills...

Or

If you were a little more effective at planning and being organised...

Sadly (or not as the case may be), I really wasn't interested in planning or organising during that part of my career. But my managers had missed the point, and also the opportunity. They were looking at themselves, as many managers do – being good at planning and organising, they were trying to project that onto me.

It would have been more effective and impactful if each year they had explored with me my:

1. Vision of success for the year.

2. Personal values.

3. Current circumstances and environment.

This would have given them a clear picture as to what my aspirations were and what was important to me. They could have challenged me on 'how' I expected to achieve my vision of success and 'what' areas I could develop to enhance my likelihood of success.

In turn, this would have enabled me to become more aware of my surroundings and then empowered me to improve in areas that would ultimately be linked to my values and vision of success.

A change of heart

There was a time in my life when my circumstances and environment changed, and planning and organising did become important to me. This was when I arrived in the world of self-employment, having left M&S Money!

Here are some of the common excuses (phrases) that I hear from people when it comes to this stage in the model:

- I don't have the time to do anything else.

- I've never been very organised.

- I find having a plan stifles me.

- I prefer to see how things work out.

- I've done OK so far in my career.

Be mindful of what you're ultimately doing when you hear yourself saying any of these phrases. Whether you accept it or not, that's entirely up to you. You are, however, resigning yourself to not achieving your vision of success.

What is the cost of not creating your Vehicle?

If you wait around expecting something to happen, don't be surprised when it doesn't. Remember Einstein's quote from earlier on, you are: 'Doing the same thing over and over again and expecting a different outcome.'

Likewise, if you approach this phase without giving it due thought, the results will be erratic at best and inconsistent. Neither are good for you, and both can contribute to you giving up if you don't think you're progressing quickly enough.

Like me, you're probably familiar with or have heard of the phrase 'Good things come to those who wait.' Now, I'll admit to being impatient at times in my life; I've wanted things to happen and to happen quickly. On occasions, though, I've had someone in my family or circle of friends share that very same phrase with me. It wasn't particularly helpful. Still, at the same time, it has seemed quite innocent and certainly with nothing sinister meant by sharing it.

Here's the thing, though; having done a quick search on this phrase, I realised that there's some confusion over who said it. Searching a little further though, I discovered that its origin traces back to the English poet Lady Mary Montgomerie Currie (1843–1905), writing under the pseudonym of Violet Fane, in her poem *'Tout Vient a Qui Sait Attendre'*:

> *All hoped-for things will come to you*
> *Who have the strength to watch an wait,*
> *Our longings spur the steeds of Fate,*
> *This has been said by one who knew.*

> *'Ah, all things come to those who wait,'*
> *(I say these words to make me glad),*
> *But something answers soft and sad,*
> *'They come, but often come too late.'*

This now starts to provoke some different thoughts. More importantly, it becomes more helpful and useful.

I've heard Miles Hilton-Barber's response (many times) to the phrase of 'the best things come to those who wait'. *'If you wait, all that you get is the leftovers from those who didn't.'*

What gets planned in, gets done and vice versa. Now, for any of you perfectionists reading this, I have a little phrase that is useful and that I use on myself: 'Done beats perfect, because perfect doesn't get done.' You may want to remember this when you're procrastinating.

How to create a Vehicle for change

You're creating a plan that both excites you and drives you every single day. If it doesn't do both of these things, then you've not got the right plan. This is absolutely not about rushing or hustling. Though there may be some changes that you are able to do or make quickly, this is very much about taking the time to get the plan right.

There are two steps to this part of the process, as outlined earlier on:

Step 1: Awareness of your current circumstances and environment.

Step 2: Creating an actionable plan that is going to work for you.

Step 1: Awareness of your current circumstances and environment

Here you're wanting to get a really clear picture of what your typical working day and week looks like. Why? You're looking for change to start to take place and at a pace. In order to do this, you have to look at what you're doing (and going to be doing) on a daily basis. Leaving things to the weekend invariably means they won't happen.

Intention, attention, distraction

This is a great exercise to discover what's happening for you and where your time and energy are currently going.

- Intention is what your focus is going to be on in relation to your vision of success.

- Attention is what you need to give your time to in order to move closer to achieving your intention.

- Distraction is what you think will prevent you from focusing or taking action.

VEHICLE EXERCISE:

Focusing on your intention, your attention and any distractions you might face

Grab the worksheet from the free Stuck workbook and fill in your answers to the following.

1. What is your intention this week (in relation to your vision of success)?

2. Where is your attention required to be in order to achieve your intention?

3. What may distract you?

However, you could look at this in a different way and ask yourself:

1. What's not getting your attention that should be (in relation to your vision of success)?

2. How can you get clearer with what your intention is?

3. What are you neglecting by allowing yourself to be distracted?

Here's an example: a salesperson who seeks to be seen as a vision of success would aim to achieve their bonus for the month/year.

What is my intention for the week?

- To achieve 15–20 leads.

Where do I need to focus my attention?

- On sticking to the process, believing in myself and going again if I get a no.

What might cause a distraction?

- Beating myself up if I get a no, looking at what others are doing, and having social media open on my laptop.

Having clarity in these three areas will set you up very differently for your day. They will also ensure that you are more productive.

Remember:

Those of you who are caught up with the daily grind, don't be surprised to see your attention going all over the place.

If you're doing something that you don't particularly enjoy, you will find distraction featuring heavily in your day. If the work that you're doing is not linked to your vision of success or values, then you're less likely to attack each day full of intent.

VEHICLE EXERCISE:

Creating your own
Daily–Weekend Tracker

Let's take a glance at the Daily–Weekend Tracker which you'll find in the Stuck workbook. Print it off, review the examples and fill your own one in.

Daily–Weekend Tracker

A TYPICAL WORKING DAY	
WAKE UP TIME	
COMMITMENTS BEFORE WORK	
LOCATION OF WORK	
WORK START TIME	
WORK FINISH TIME	
COMMITMENTS AFTER WORK	
SLEEP TIME	

A TYPICAL WEEKEND	
WAKE UP TIME	
PERSONAL COMMITMENTS	
WORK COMMITMENTS	
SLEEP TIME	

Having completed the Daily–Weekend Tracker, what do you notice from the answers you've provided? Here's an example: Co-owner and Director of a Lighting Company:

Daily–Weekend Tracker

A TYPICAL WORKING DAY	
WAKE UP TIME	5:30–6:30
COMMITMENTS BEFORE WORK	Children up and ready to go for childminders' drop off 7:30 (if my week is tough and lots of commitments then I might try and run in the mornings, but this will mean waking up before the kids to do so, 4:30–5:00ish)
LOCATION OF WORK	Winchester or on the road for meetings

181

WORK START TIME	8:00–8:30, depending on who is doing the drop off (my wife or myself)
WORK FINISH TIME	16:30–18:00, depending on the children's pick up and work commitments
COMMITMENTS AFTER WORK	Spend time with the children up to bedtime (19:00–19:30) then run after bedtime
SLEEP TIME	22:00–23:00

A typical weekend

WAKE UP TIME	5:30–6:30 one day and a lie in the other (my wife and I have a lie in each at the weekend)
PERSONAL COMMITMENTS	Clubs for the boys. Try and do a park run on a Saturday and try not to run for too long on the weekend. Family day out one day or catch up with friends and family
WORK COMMITMENTS	None
SLEEP TIME	22:00–23:00

If we look at the example above, we can deduce a few things:

1. Family time is important to them and they choose to switch off from work at the weekends.

2. They have a similar wake up and sleep time each day.

3. Running is an important part of their life.

At a glance, this tracker allows you to see where your time and energy are currently going, and it will also confirm what your commitments are as well. On reflection, you may already be considering what you want to change. This is important as you start to look at what you can change to allow you to move forward towards your vision of success.

It's only a glance, though. As you're about to see, there tends to be a lot more going on in each of our lives. With that in mind, let's take a deeper look at other factors that may or may not be impacting your circumstances and environment. This is done by completing the Priorities Tracker below.

VEHICLE EXERCISE:

Building your own Priorities Tracker

This tool is also in your free Stuck resource page. Print it out and work through this series of poignant questions to get you to think about your priorities.

Priorities Tracker

HOME LIFE:

What are your responsibilities outside of work, e.g. partner, parent, carer, volunteer, hobbies etc.?

WORK LIFE:

What are your responsibilities inside of work, e.g. leader, manager, mentor, committee member etc.?

PHYSICAL:

What activities do you do and how frequently, e.g. running, swimming, football, walking etc.?

MENTAL:

What activities do you do and how frequently, e.g. mindfulness, meditation, journaling etc.?

SLEEP AND RECOVERY:

What is your typical number of hours sleep during a 24-hour cycle, including naps?

LIFESTYLE:

What does your diet typically include/exclude and how does this differ in work versus at home?

* * *

Having completed the Priorities Tracker, what do you notice from the answers you've provided?

Continuing with the Co-owner and Director of a Lighting Company, let's share his answers:

Priorities Tracker

HOME LIFE:

What are your responsibilities outside of work, e.g. partner, parent, carer, volunteer, hobbies etc.?

Husband and father are my main priorities, with running as a very important hobby for me.

WORK LIFE:

What are your responsibilities inside of work, e.g. leader, manager, mentor, committee member etc.?

All of the above. As you can imagine, as a co-owner in a business, I have to take up responsibility in all aspects of what we do.

PHYSICAL:

What activities do you do and how frequently, e.g. running, swimming, football, walking etc.?

Running 3–4 times a week, bike 1 day a week, strength training 1 day a week.

MENTAL:

What activities do you do and how frequently, e.g. mindfulness, meditation, journaling etc.?

None.

SLEEP AND RECOVERY:

What is your typical number of hours sleep during a 24-hour cycle including naps?

7–8 hours.

LIFESTYLE:

What does your diet typically include/exclude and how does this differ in work versus at home?

My diet is pretty mixed, but it could do with being a little healthier from a portion perspective. I eat convenience foods when in the office or on the go.

If we look at the example above, we can now deduce a few more things:

1. Family, work and running are core to this person and trying to balance these is important to them.

2. Less importance is currently placed upon their mental health in comparison to their physical health.

3. Lifestyle is mixed and may become a consideration when going through any change.

In any situation, it's important to consider the impact that change may have on your current environment and circumstances. Here we can see that family will be an important part of supporting any change and a consideration when creating an actionable plan.

It's fair to say that we all experience a certain amount of pressure to fulfil all aspects of our lives. Society expects, and social media fuels, the desire for a perfect life. In reality, it simply doesn't work that way. On completing these two trackers, you may feel compelled to make other changes to your work or lifestyle and that's OK. See them as a bonus to the work you've already committed to by going through this process.

As in the previous chapter, it's really important to know where you're starting from. This increased conscious level of awareness certainly helps before you start the planning part of this stage.

Step 2: Creating an actionable plan that is going to work for you

The work you've completed so far has been building up to this point. It's worth reminding you and restating that you're clear on your vision of success and know where you're starting from. You've also established some steps that will move you closer towards achieving your vision of success.

In relation to your important values, you know what these are. You also know which (if any) of your top five values need addressing. You've also got a clear picture of your current circumstances and environment, so now let's get to work on a plan.

VEHICLE EXERCISE:

Developing your own action plan

The skeleton of your action plan can be found in your free Stuck workbook. Print it out then...

1. At the top of it, write down your vision of success, including the date of its achievement.

2. Underneath this, write down where you are currently in relation to this and put today's date next to it.

3. Start to write down a list of all the tasks that (you think) need to be done to move you forward from where you are currently.

4. Out of all of the tasks, highlight or circle the top three tasks that will move you forward the most. (Note: these aren't the easy ones or quick wins. Often these are the hardest ones and may take some time.)

5. Decide which of those top three tasks you're going to tackle first.

6. Plan your top task into your calendar and allocate time against it.

7. Repeat Step 6 with your other top three tasks.

8. Share your top three tasks with whoever needs to know, based on your answers to the home/work life priorities tracker. (These people form part of your support team and this will be explained more in the Voice chapter.)

9. Do the work (however long it takes) and complete task one.

10. Repeat with tasks two and three.

Note: the significance of beginning with the harder tasks is that, once completed, they will move you on the most. We are wired to choose the easy tasks and cheat ourselves into believing that we're making progress. All the while, though, the harder tasks get overlooked and pushed to one side.

Once you've completed your top task, you have momentum. You also have increased your own belief and so more confidence starts to follow. Completing tasks two and three will make you feel almost invincible and, as a coach, this is one of the most rewarding things that I get to see on a regular basis.

The bank employee who dreamed of becoming an online marketer

Back in July 2011, a good friend and ex-colleague of mine from M&S Money got in touch and asked if I was taking on any new clients at that time. There had just been a big announcement made by the leadership team of another big bank in Chester; they were going to be making over 100 people redundant and his team was one of the areas being considered for redundancies.

He was working alongside a lady who was considering her options, including looking at setting up her own business. Straight away he'd suggested to her that she should consider having a conversation with me. As a coach and someone running their own business, he thought I would be able to help her. I was happy for him to pass on my details and agreed that we'd have an initial discussion.

Within 24 hours, I'd received a call from her, and she proceeded to share with me some of her story. She wasn't particularly happy doing the job she was doing, and the 30-minute commute every day each way wasn't helping. In addition, she had a young family to think about. However, this impending redundancy had come at a good time so, to be fair to her, she'd already started to view this positively. She had already begun familiarising herself in the area of online marketing, and she was doing some low-level writing and work producing pay-per-click articles.

We agreed to meet up the following week. This gave her time to complete some pre-work prior to our first face-to-face meeting. I usually set potential new clients a small challenge prior to meeting them for the first time. This allows me to gauge their level of commitment, but it also gives them an insight into how I work and my expectations.

I asked her to give some thought as to what she wanted to do in the future; she had to form her vision of success. I also asked her to consider her 'why' for wanting to do this. Finally, I asked that she make some notes and bring them with her.

Very quickly, it became apparent that what really excited her and fired her up was the possibility of working for herself. She'd risen to the challenge and completed all of the pre-work prior to our meeting; this would bode well. The work she was doing for the bank wasn't motivating or stimulating her; it was a means to an end and allowed her to provide for her young family. As the business would no longer be requiring her services in her current role, and she had no desire to transfer to another department, we set to work.

Her vision of success was to run her own online marketing company. She wanted to be doing this by April the following year as this coincided with her date of leaving the bank. This gave her (and me) just under eight months to achieve her goals. More importantly, she was determined to be earning the same income (if not more) from her business come April 2012.

Within the pre-work, she'd started to put together a bit of a plan. It resembled more of a 'to-do list' initially, but I was pleased, nonetheless. We talked about the tasks she'd need to do, and we agreed a plan to meet up every two to three weeks to review her progress and look ahead.

The first few sessions followed a similar pattern. She would arrive and give me an update of the work she'd completed, then we'd talk about any of the challenges that she faced and explore ways to work through them. Finally, we'd look at what tasks were outstanding, and she'd leave each session happy and also clear on what she was going to do next. She was getting through a great deal of work, whilst also doing her day job and looking after the family requirements.

Driving home after one particular session, something wasn't sitting right in my mind. You know when things are almost too good to be true? I'll admit that she was progressing along nicely, so I wondered what it could be, and then it dawned upon me. After each session, she was choosing to do the easier tasks, or so I thought. They were the ones she'd had experience of or had some familiarity with.

At the next session, I chose a different approach. She updated me on what she'd completed since the previous session, and I still couldn't fault her work ethic and determination. She'd also brought along several pieces of paper with tasks that she still had outstanding, so here was my opportunity. I asked her to spend five minutes looking over all of the outstanding tasks and to highlight the top three that would move her on the most, once she'd completed them.

The top three tasks were huge and would require her to spend a lot more time, researching them and getting familiar with what they required, as she'd not done them before. I suggested that we change our frequency of meeting and not meet up again until she had completed them. She agreed and left with a new plan.

I didn't hear from her for over a month! I genuinely thought I'd either upset her or angered her. Then one day an email came through, saying that she'd completed the top three tasks and asking if we could meet up again.

The shift in terms of her belief and confidence, having tucked herself away for nearly six weeks working on this, was unbelievable. Everything else quickly fell into place and there would be no future tasks that she couldn't now do. It was shortly afterwards that we turned our focus and attention to generating income.

She started that calendar year with a projected income for January, building through February and March and leading up to her leaving date in April. Her vision of success was to achieve the same income that she'd been earning at the bank whilst working for herself and working from home. I'm pleased to say that she exceeded her own expectations.

Today, she continues to run her own business and provide advice, guidance and training to other SMEs across the UK and abroad.

Personal reflection

I don't know what's happening in your life right now. As you've read through this chapter, I wonder how many excuses you've come up with as to why you can't do something or why the time isn't right at the moment. I often hear the classic line, 'I'd love to but...'

Perhaps you have got yourself into a situation where you're just too busy, and busyness may have become a metric for determining your success. There's a whole load of busyness happening in the world of work right now and we are seeing the implications of this in relation to people's health and wellbeing. In some organisations, people wear the 'busyness badge' like a badge of honour. They can't wait to tell you how busy they are when you ask them how they are doing.

Busyness, by design, keeps you firmly where you are right now. Your circumstances don't change, but your quality of life slowly declines. You don't notice it at first, or if you do, you play it down, but it's real and I implore you to not only take notice, but to take action.

As Dr Jeffrey Pfeffer points out in his book, *Dying for a Paycheck*: 'Because employers see long work hours as a signal of employee effort and loyalty, employers reward those who put in the long hours.' This is systemic in organisations and contributes to busyness, as employees see this as the way to get on and forward their career.

He goes on to share that: 'People get trapped in a variety of ways, into staying in harmful work environments.' However: 'Leaders should ensure that at the end of each day, their employees return home in good shape, prepared to live fulfilled lives outside of work.' Sadly, it may before some time for organisations adopt this approach. Don't wait for your organisation to change, or for the leaders within your organisation to realise the impacts of a 'busyness culture' where employees feel stuck.

Be proactive. Work through the exercises included in this chapter (if you haven't already) and see where your time and energy are currently going. The results themselves will provide you with discussion points that you can then share with the important people in your life and also with your manager.

— Key takeaways

- Before you jump ahead and start coming up with a plan, stop and allow yourself to understand more about your circumstances and current environment.

- Be mindful of what distractions you allow into your day because they will ultimately take you away from your vision of success.

- The time that you ultimately dedicate to this stage of the model will be paid back in dividends.

- Do the hard tasks first to get your momentum going and then the easy ones will take care of themselves.

— Questions to consider

1. What can you change about your current circumstances or environment today to create time in your calendar?

2. What are your top three tasks that will move you on the most once you've completed them?

3. Who can you share your plan with to gain more support from or act as an accountability buddy?

4. Who do you know who is doing something similar already (to your vision of success) and who you can learn from?

5. How will you feel as you start to take steps towards (and get closer to) achieving your vision of success?

CHAPTER 11

WITH VALOUR, EVERY BUMP IS AN OPPORTUNITY

'Don't let the force of an impression when it first hits you knock you off your feet; just say to it: hold on a moment, let me see who you are and what you represent. Let me put you to the test.'

EPICTETUS

What is Valour?

Valour can make all the difference; I've witnessed it over and over again with my own eyes, and I've heard it through the tone of those determined to achieve something in their life. The word valour itself comes from the Latin word *'valere'*, which means to be strong. Valour is to show great courage in the face of danger, especially in battle.

Whilst you may not be going into battle, at times you may have to fight for what you want to achieve. There is no straight path, and you will almost certainly experience bumps in the road on your journey towards achieving your vision of success.

You will need to show courage, as you execute the plan which you have created, and you will need to draw on some inner strength and be disciplined, so as not to be tempted along the way by easy options or quick life hacks. Worthwhile change takes time. If you consider your vision of success to be a worthwhile change, then there will be moments ahead when your valour will be challenged and tested.

Acceptance and patience, as outlined earlier on in Chapter 5, will also serve you well alongside valour as you begin to make your vision of success your reality.

Why is Valour so important?

'It is not the critic who counts; not the man who points out how the strong man stumbles, or where the doer of deeds could have done better. The credit belongs to the man who is actually in the arena, whose face is marred by dust and sweat and blood; who strives valiantly; who

—❝—

The hardest and most important step along your journey is the first step, but it's only hard because you perceive it to be so.

—❞—

errs, who comes short again and again, because there is no effort without error and shortcoming; but who does actually strive to do the deeds; who knows great enthusiasm, the great devotions; of high achievement, and who at the worst, if he fails, at least fails while daring greatly, so that his place shall never be with those cold and timid souls who neither know victory nor defeat.'

THEODORE ROOSEVELT – 'THE MAN IN THE ARENA'

Valour moves us forward in every aspect of our life, and it is crucial in this instance for two reasons:

1. It gets you moving and taking the first step.
2. It keeps you going when you're faced with adversity.

1. Get moving

It is said that many people live their life within their comfort zone. The main reason being because it's comfortable, but it also comes with limitations. Cast your mind back to Chapter 2 when we discussed what it's like when you're stuck in a rut or going through the daily grind. Choosing to do nothing other than staying in the rut or in a place where you feel stuck, keeps you firmly in that comfort zone.

Finding some valour – and it's in there believe me – is what gets you started. The hardest and most important step along your journey is the first step, but it's only hard because you perceive it to be so. That's why you build it up and make it out to be something it isn't.

Fear kicks in, as we discussed in Chapter 5, and then your comfort zone all of a sudden becomes appealing.

Fact: the first step is rarely as scary or daunting as you make out in your own mind.

The manager who contemplated a new career

Usually, when I facilitate development programmes, I will be invited to go out with the group in the evening. I often politely decline, unless it's the final evening of a programme. However, on one particular evening, I accepted and joined the group for the evening meal.

They didn't have a table big enough to accommodate us all, so one manager had the pleasure of having dinner with just me! He'd opened up at different points during the programme and we had developed a good rapport.

During dinner he happened to mention to me that he was considering leaving the business and setting up his own venture in Spain. I was curious to hear more and it transpired that he wanted to set up a business selling pre-made cocktail mixes to bars and hotels. His father was already living in Spain and had the capital and connections to support his idea. He was full of energy and excitement as he described his idea to me, but this was going to be a huge leap for him and I could see he was apprehensive and nervous.

He wasn't yet 100% sure, so doubt was creeping in – but not about his idea, or even raising some capital. The doubt centred around whether it could be done from a manufacturing perspective.

So, I asked him a question: 'What would you need to discover and understand in order for the manufacturing phase to be possible?' This, in turn, would open up the opportunity for everything else to fall into place.

He went on his way in search of some answers. Two weeks prior to the next workshop he contacted me to tell me that he wouldn't be attending. He'd found the courage to take the first step and discovered a manufacturer who would work with him in Spain. Once he'd taken the first step and got moving, there was nothing stopping him. He left the organisation shortly afterwards, and the last I heard he was still running a business in Spain.

'He who suffers before it is necessary suffers more than is necessary.'

SENECA THE YOUNGER

2. Keep going

Once you get going, keeping going becomes the key. In many cases, you will have demonstrated valour to get started; in other cases, you will have just got on with what you had been putting off. However, valour doesn't go away in a box and not come out again; it is the answer to most of your fears, so I suggest you keep it with you at all times. It takes you to new places and allows you to build momentum, plus, it's never as scary as what you tell yourself.

Valour is part of you and always has been, from the moment you started to crawl, right up until now. You've been choosing your moments of valour carefully throughout your life. More than ever before, it's going to be required on this journey; your journey towards achieving your vision of success.

Example: The Planning Manager (story in Chapter 6)

A short reminder of her situation: She wasn't happy and found herself plodding at work and generally stuck at life; in fact, her life was work, in the main. She didn't have a clear vision (or so she thought) and had no idea about her values. Her manager wasn't particularly helpful, but then he didn't really know how to help; he only told her that she needed to work on her confidence!

Step 1

We agreed to explore 'her need to work on her confidence' and came up with some work situations where she could be proactive and project confidence. The first step to get her going would be for her to provide her manager with a morning update of progress from the previous day. For some time, this had been initiated by her manager asking her for an update. This one simple task would require valour and demonstrate her being more confident in the eyes of her manager.

Step 2

To keep her moving forward with her confidence, we then looked at her doing the following:

- Providing updates in team meetings.

- Getting up from her desk and going to speak to colleagues instead of emailing them.

- Questioning colleagues for further information to allow her to gain a better understanding of how she could support them with their workload.

- Delegating tasks to her line report.

- Saying no (with an explanation as to why) to requests from colleagues that fell outside of her role and responsibilities.

Within the space of a month, she was showing more valour and making good progress. She told me that she was feeling more confident. Her manager, however, was still saying she needed to be more confident. I asked her to share some examples with me of when she was interacting with her manager, in the hope that this would provide insight into when he was perceiving a lack of confidence from her.

Quickly she reeled off several examples. Bingo. We narrowed it down to:

- Presentations to office colleagues, which she wasn't very confident doing.

- Town hall/community meetings, which she allowed a colleague to lead.

- Providing updates to the directors, which she shied away from.

Over the next few sessions, we would talk about her progress, focusing primarily on her confidence and the moments of valour that she'd shown. We also discussed her manager and his perception of her confidence. Lo and behold, this had changed!

As she'd become more confident; he'd recognised the difference as well. He had stopped telling her that she 'needed to work on her confidence' and started telling her to 'be more assertive'. She rose to the challenge once more, and I'll let you draw your own conclusions as to how this turned out for her by revisiting Chapter 6.

Valour can be the difference.

See whatever obstacles are in your way as bumps in the road. As you've learned already, if something is in your way, it becomes part of the way. You don't avoid it or put it off; you embrace it and work out a way. Making valour a part of everyday life is something each of us can do and I'll share how you can do this later on in the chapter.

What is the cost of lacking Valour?

The cost of **not** choosing to be valiant is that you inevitably fail. You may view this as not failing because you haven't done anything, but that's a failure in itself. You remain where you are, doing what you're doing, stuck or in the daily grind, with this compounded by the fact that your vision of success is just a dream after all.

Remember the voice in your head? The one that says: 'Are you sure you want to do that?', 'What if you fail or it doesn't work out?' and 'What will others think or say?' You allow the voice in your head to win, every time you choose not to be valiant.

Mark Manson shares a story about Picasso in his book, *The Subtle Art of Not Giving a Fuck*. The message within this story is: 'Improvement at anything is based on thousands of tiny failures, and the magnitude of your success is based on how many times you've failed at something.'

Armed with valour, you're more likely to be courageous when things fail, just like Picasso. Sometimes it works out and on other occasions it doesn't. When it doesn't, see these as tiny failures that will ultimately lead you closer to achieving success.

Do you really want to give up the dream of achieving your vision of success? Put to one side the work that you've already done? Accept that this only happens to other people? Of course you don't, and why should you?

Being aware of the cost of **not** being valiant or showing up each day armed with valour is something you need to be mindful of, because it's real. But this isn't new to you. You're likely to know the phrase 'Fortune favours the brave.' This comes from the Goddess of luck, Fortuna.

How to use Valour to move forward

People will often say to me, 'I wish I had your confidence.' This is usually followed up by them saying, 'If I had more confidence, I'd...'

- just go for it.

- do this or that.

- take more risks.

- not worry so much.

Well, the truth is, I haven't always had the confidence that I have today. I was that child aged seven who got a question wrong in class. My teacher was actually Miss Rowlands too! Throughout my schooling, confidence didn't come easily or naturally. For most of my childhood, I was referred to as the quiet child.

You see, I was like you. In many ways I'm still that quiet, shy boy.

I don't mind letting you in on a secret; my confidence has been learned. What I mean is that I've had to learn how to project confidence outwardly. Some people would refer to this as 'Faking it until you make it.' I'm not a big fan of this phrase, though I understand that its intention is to empower you to practise being confident (in this scenario) until you become confident.

Over many years, I've deliberately chosen to learn through practising, by making mistakes and ultimately failing many times. I have built up my confidence through little acts of courage (or valour), without which I wouldn't be doing what I'm doing today. If I hadn't been courageous and shown valour I'd still be at M&S Money.

In essence, I did it by doing some of what I call the 'scary things'. Scary things are things that made me a little anxious, I hadn't done before, or I didn't have any knowledge about. Some of those scary things for me included:

- Sitting at the front during presentations.

- Asking questions in a meeting.

- Challenging colleagues to gain a better understanding of their points.

- Volunteering to demonstrate a roleplay situation.

- Requesting a meeting with a senior leader (Andy Ripley) and asking him to be my mentor.

Two things happened when I started doing scary things each day:

1. My inner confidence and belief in myself grew.

2. Others started commenting on how confident and brave I was.

This will be the same for you. If you want to become more confident, start doing what confident people do.

In relation to your action plan that you have created from the previous chapter, here's how you can help yourself to move forward.

VALOUR EXERCISE:

Facing the scary things

Now return to your action plan:

1. Highlight the tasks on your action plan that scare you the most. The ones that you see as being bumps in the road along your journey.

2. Choose one task to focus on initially.

3. In relation to this task, write down in your journal:

   - something that you will do straightaway (that's easy but scary).

   - something that you will do with a bit more consideration (not as easy but scary).

   - something that you will do that is really big and bold (and scary).

4. Set a deadline to complete each task in Step 3.

5. Ask yourself, who do you know that can help/support you with this?

6. Complete.

7. Reflect on what you've learned from this experience.

Being made redundant in 2014

I was determined to set up my own company once more, even though it hadn't worked out successfully the first time around. Emma and I had spoken about this many times, even before I was made redundant. She knew how much it meant to me to be doing work that I loved.

So, this is something I did straight away:

- On the way home from work, having just received the dreaded news, I rang the people I knew who were working in the L&D space.

Something I did with a bit more consideration:

- Within a few days I wrote out a list of all the people who I knew who might be able to help me in some way achieve my vision of success. I didn't know at the time, but this would become my daily work list over the next six to seven weeks.

Something I did that was big and bold:

- I reached out to thought leaders who I admired and followed on social media and asked for their advice and, if possible, some of their time. I was amazed by some of their responses and I was delighted and excited to speak with people like Jim Lawless, the author of *Taming Tigers*.

My own learning and confidence from being valiant went through the roof, although reaching out and speaking to people in my network, including Kirsty Mac, Kevin McAlpin and Steve Adams, took some guts for me. I was opening up and asking for help, as everything seemed scary and new for me, and sending messages on social media to some of my 'heroes' like Jim (as I've mentioned), Mike Pegg and Miles Hilton-Barber was a big leap of faith. Every conversation or message led to something else – a follow-up, an introduction, a meeting.

Even an old colleague who I'd managed in my M&S Money days, Debbie Lawrence, came back to me with a suggestion. That suggestion led to a meeting and presentation to her boss, Emma Davis, who I would go on to facilitate work for at Specsavers. To this day, we've kept in touch and have worked together many times since Emma went solo and set up her own L&D company. Because of my experience over those six to seven weeks, I always encourage others to do something similar.

Your reflection is so valuable here because it demonstrates to you what you can do. It builds confidence and also encourages you to keep moving forward with the other tasks on your action plan.

The Deputy Store Manager who shared his ambitions

Back in 2012 I was facilitating training for managers at a mobile phone retailer. The demographic of managers in the organisation at the time was generally 20–25. They were full of energy, enthusiasm and excitement to be working in an industry with the latest technology.

Amongst every training group, there were typically 90–95% of managers who wanted to progress towards running their own stores. Some also had an eye on progressing to regional or area director roles in the future, but the competition and rivalry was intense on every training programme. I could have some fun in relation to the vision of success with the deputy store managers, especially those who wanted to become store managers.

With every new group, I would always ask them what their vision of success was. Having already provided some insight, you could probably guess what the standard answer was. A deputy manager would answer, a store manager. A store manager would answer, a regional manager. And so on. The development path was clearly laid out for any aspiring manager. However, there were a limited number of stores and therefore a limited number of opportunities.

Like with any clear vision of success, there has to be an achievement date. Pretty much every aspiring deputy manager that I trained wanted to become a store manager as soon as possible. You can already see the problem with this, although many of them couldn't.

The challenge I posed to them was: how well does your area director know you? I elaborated by sharing that if they don't know you or what your intentions are – e.g. your vision of success – then you are not on their radar. If you're not on their radar, by definition, that means that you are off their radar. I'd then suggest that this is what you must address, and I'd deliberately leave them to ponder on this.

Typically, I'd get some challenge and push back, followed by a host of reasons and excuses as to why their area director didn't know them well enough at this stage. However, for one particular manager, this had resonated with him, so he stopped behind to speak to me at the end of the first day. He was ambitious and driven and he'd been thinking about this, but he didn't really know what to do.

When I asked him what he thought he could do, he responded with:

- I could catch up with my area director the next time he's in store.

- If (not when) he speaks to me, I could tell him about my aspirations.

- I can pass this course and share my intentions with them during my presentation in three to four

months' time. (This was required for the end of programme sign off.)

- In the meantime, I could tell my store manager again about my ambition.

He was coming up with the easy responses, the same responses that every other deputy store manager had. These weren't necessarily going to help him, so he needed to change his thinking. He was missing some valour.

His vision of success at that moment in time was to become a store manager within 12 months, so he didn't have time to waste. His area director didn't know him as he was only a few months into joining the organisation.

So, I challenged him to think about what would move him on the quickest, and I asked – if he was being courageous, what would he do? He paused for a moment to consider this. His body language was also telling me that he was a little reluctant. Area directors can be intimidating, and they often were in this organisation. I was feeling for him. When he started to speak again, I could hear from his tone that he was clearly apprehensive. Then he just came out and said, 'I'll call him and ask him for a meeting to discuss my future (vision of success).'

Nodding and smiling to myself, I said, 'That sounds like a good idea, you should do that.' Not wanting to give him too much time to worry or stress over it, I said, 'So when can you call him?'

He told me that he would text him that evening (as he didn't want to disturb him) and agree a convenient time the following day to have an initial chat about the programme and his future. The following morning, he headed straight for me to share his news. He'd shown some valour and taken the first step. He'd spoken to his area director on the way into the training, and this was swiftly followed up by a meeting that week when he returned into store.

By the time we met again for the next workshop, he was well and truly on his area director's radar. The training programme concluded with a presentation from each deputy manager to their area director. This was another opportunity for him to influence his director and shine.

I remember arriving at the Reading store on the morning of the final presentations and being met by the Deputy Manager when I signed in. He looked excited and nervous at the same time; he was smiling and couldn't wait to share with me his idea for his final presentation. I couldn't believe it when he told me that he planned to open up his presentation by asking his director, the HR Manager and myself to join in and do 'The Birdie Song'.

Wow, I thought, that takes guts. If he was feeling that valiant then I owed it to him to play my part.

His presentation went like a dream. He received brilliant feedback from his area director and HR Manager. Within a month of delivering his presentation, he turned up on the store managers' programme with one of my colleagues, after which he received a promotion to become a store manager.

On reflection, he could have chosen the easy option and sat it out and waited until someone noticed him, but who's to say if anyone ever would have done? A little bit of valour goes a long way.

'Believe that you can and you're halfway there.'

THEODORE ROOSEVELT

Personal reflection

The truth is that every big decision in your life is a brave decision. Where to go to university, which company to join, who to marry etc. I know 100% that I wouldn't be doing what I'm doing today if I hadn't been courageous and made some brave decisions in my life. There hasn't just been one courageous moment either; there have been many along the way, during my career in the corporate world and subsequently since choosing to be self-employed.

The easy choices and decisions we face in our lives always seem to be, easier! They are tempting and usually within our reach. It's also worth noting that, in my own life, there have been times when I've not chosen to be courageous, because I've told myself that it was easier to do something else. As I look back on those occasions, things didn't change in any way for me and only caused me more frustration and pain later on.

Here's a quote to reflect on for a moment:

'Hard choices, easy life.
Easy choices, hard life.'

JERZY GREGOREK

Jerzy framed this quote to explain his journey from alcoholism to Olympic weightlifting glory. In the process, he also became a world champion and a world record holder. The origin of his quote comes from Stoic philosophy and this was used by Tim Ferriss in his TED talk to support the use of his own fear setting process.

It's helpful because it reminds us all that those difficult decisions are worth making as they are leading you towards your vision of success and, ultimately, an easier life. If I hadn't shown courage in leaving M&S Money and setting up my own business in 2010, I wouldn't necessarily have been as courageous in setting up another business when I was made redundant in 2014.

By simply reaching this point in the process, you will have already come up with your vehicle for bringing about change. As I've stated many times, the biggest thing holding any of us back is our thoughts. Keep challenging yourself every day and every week to do the courageous stuff; the rewards will follow your hard work.

——Key takeaways ——————————

- Fortune favours the brave, so go and show some valour today.

- Think about the day-to-day opportunities where you can be courageous and start doing some brave things.

- Valour is like compound interest – the more you are courageous, the bigger the payback.

- The reality of what you're scared of is never as bad as your imagination.

——Questions to consider ——————

1. What are you putting off doing? Think of something that a bit of valour could help you with.

2. What are the big things that you'd really like to do, but are scared of?

3. Who can you approach to give you a nudge?

4. Where can you bring moments of courage into your day?

5. How will you feel as your confidence starts to grow? What else will this allow you to do in the future?

CHAPTER 12

— USE THE VOICE:— HOW TO GET BY WITH A LITTLE HELP FROM YOUR FRIENDS

'Our job in this life is not to shape ourselves into some ideal we imagine we ought to be, but to find out who we already are and become it.'

STEVEN PRESSFIELD – THE WAR OF ART

What is the Voice?

The voice is twofold. Firstly, it refers to your own voice and your confidence to share your ideas with others. Secondly, it's how you can amplify this by carefully choosing the voices that you surround yourself with.

A quick test:

Ask yourself the following question: when was the last time that you achieved something significant (like your vision of success or an important goal) <u>completely</u> on your own? Honestly now. You didn't even get a tiny bit of help from anyone? Come on! Really? Without any help or support from others? If you have, then great for you.

In most cases, though, we achieve better results or outcomes when working with others. Like the many examples throughout this book, people have sought the voices of others, utilising their support and guidance at different points along their journey. Right now, your voice on its own may not be enough.

Cast your mind back to the earlier chapters when we explored your inner voice. Yes, this voice can talk you up, especially when you're needing to show some valour, but we also know that this voice can talk you out of things that are new or scary and convince you to put certain things off.

During this stage of the process, you'll be encouraged to use your voice and share your plan with others so that they can help support you in achieving your vision of success. To be clear, though, you will still do the majority of the work needed to bring about change, but you'll be able to draw on other people and feel like you're not having to go it alone.

I've previously talked about the importance of others, whether that's working with a coach or having someone who can act as an accountability buddy. In this chapter, I'll show you how to:

1. Challenge your inner voice to confidently tell people what you're doing.

2. Create your own personal board, similar to that of an executive board committee in an organisation, where you are able to draw on voices other than your own.

Note: the idea of a 'personal board' is a concept and doesn't require you to set up an actual board!

Why is the Voice so important?

Valour gets you started and keeps you going in your quest to achieve your vision of success. The voice is what allows you to have the conversations you need to move forward, as well as making sure it is not about being alone. The voice also gets you over the line and celebrating your achievement.

The voice stage is so important because it says two things:

1. 'Hey, world! This is what I'm doing. I'm serious about it and I am ready.'

2. 'OK, I don't have to do this all by myself.'

Just these two thoughts can be encouraging and hugely empowering: let's be honest, doing everything on your own, without the support of others, is daunting for many people.

This is also why some of you don't even consider entertaining thoughts of creating your own vision of success, as the feeling of being alone and not knowing who to turn to puts some of you off going through change. Your inner voice talks you out of it, even before you've mentioned it as a possible idea to someone.

That's not you, though, and it's not going to happen to you; you're going to finish what you've started, and you're going to do it by surrounding yourself with the voices of others. How can I be so sure? Well, if you've arrived at this point in the book and got yourself through to the final part of the model, then the omens are very positive indeed.

To get to this point, you will have already started to use your voice and share your vision of success with your partner, close friends and some family members. They tend to be the ones who you turn to first. They're also the ones who love you the most and want to see you happy. On occasions, they've probably been the ones on the receiving end of a frustrated, unhappy, yet much needed download after you've experienced a miserable day at work.

All of these are positive signs of your voice getting louder and stronger. This is a change that's seen you move from apathy and denial to one of clear focus and intent.

In the case of those working for organisations, many of you will have spoken to your manager as well. Not just about your vision of success but also your important personal values. You may have instigated this yourself or simply taken the opportunity with your last appraisal to shed some light upon the things that have been going through your mind.

Here's a reminder. You can also use this as a way of reviewing how far you've come as well!

When the problem doesn't exist!

- You have a clear vision of success and you've been using this template for some time.

- Your vision of success is what you've been working towards and it provides you with purpose in your life and meaning in the work you do.

- Alongside this vision of success, you and your boss are aware of the important values in your life and how these are aligned to your vision of success and valued in the company and the work you're doing right now. (If this hasn't happened for you, then you may be having the realisation that you need to leave.)

- Values are what drive you to get out of bed in the morning, and they are the behaviours that your boss and work colleagues get to see each day (if they choose to notice).

As a result of these things, the work you're doing won't actually feel like work.

What is the cost of not amplifying your Voice?

The likely cost in your case is nothing changes for you. I say 'likely' because, whilst there's a chance that you could do all the work on your own and achieve your vision of success, the reality is very few people do. Very few get to where they want to be without help from those around them, without opportunities that come out of conversations with those people in their networks. In those cases, they're not tapping into this huge resource – which could be mobilised to their benefit if they stopped trying to do it all on their own. Because of this shut-off approach, they are cutting their potential growth short.

It's really hard on your own; to have that discipline and drive and determination to keep going when it gets tough – and it does get tough – is difficult. I've tried and failed many times. Where I and others have had the most success is when we've worked with a coach and reached out to others for guidance and support.

The themes that are covered in this book aren't small changes that anyone could make to their lives tomorrow. If small changes were all it took for people to get unstuck or move away from the daily grind, then more people would be engaged with the work that they're currently doing, and the simple fact is that they're not.

You've shared with your loved ones and those closest to you already. If you don't take the opportunity to share with the wider world and the important people in your life, then how can they possibly support you and fully get behind your dreams with you? If you don't take the opportunity to speak to your manager, then sadly they will continue to view you and your ambitions the same way as they do currently.

'Fortune favours the brave' remember?

Here's a reminder from the very beginning of the book as to what you're accepting by not choosing to amplify your voice.

When the problem does exist (an example of a typical day, as provided in the opening chapter):

- You feel stuck.

- You go to work, yet it isn't working.

- You're in the grind that many employees and managers face each day.

- It doesn't end when you log off at work and head home either.

- You're spending part of your evening (and weekend) responding to emails or completing work tasks.

- You even tell yourself that, by catching up at home, you're getting ahead for the following day or week!

You don't want to choose this and here's how to make sure that you don't.

—"—

Let's listen to and challenge your 'inner voice'.

—"—

How to use the Voice to maximum effect

Remember the approach to the voice is twofold.

1. Listen to and challenge your inner voice.

2. Create your own personal board, similar to that of an executive board committee in an organisation.

Step 1: Listen to and challenge your inner voice

If you happen to find that there's some fear creeping back into your thoughts, then go back to Chapter 5 and work through some of the suggestions on how to tackle those fears. The inner critic in our minds never truly goes away, but you can quieten it.

Firstly then, let's listen to and challenge your 'inner voice'. You can do this by sharing with your 'inner voice' some important truths. For example, your inner voice might say, 'I don't think you're going to be able to pull this off, you probably shouldn't bother wasting your time.'

TRUTH 1: VISION

'Hang on a minute. I've done the work and created a clear vision of success that is linked to my important personal values and I'm excited by this.'

Inner voice: 'I'm just not sure about this and I don't even know why you get out of bed in the morning.'

TRUTH 2: VALUES

'That's just not true. I am absolutely clear on the values that are important to me and I'm not going to compromise on these anymore.'

Inner voice: 'Really it's OK – no, it's not. It's OK – no, it's not. Oh, you're just making a fuss over nothing.'

TRUTH 3: VIEW

'Woah there. Things have been like this for a while and that promised change hasn't happened. I'm stepping up and taking control of changing this.'

Inner voice: 'You're rubbish at planning and, besides, you have so much other stuff going on right now.'

TRUTH 4: VEHICLE

'Just a moment. I have created an exciting and actionable plan and I'm already doing stuff to change my situation.'

Inner voice: 'This bravery thing isn't you and you're better off giving up and going back to what you were doing.'

TRUTH 5: VALOUR

'Stop right there. I have started being brave already and taking small steps. I can feel my confidence slowly growing and this is allowing me to be more courageous.'

Inner voice: 'Remember the time you did something brave and it didn't work out. That could happen again.'

It's impossible to cover here every possible thought that your inner voice will throw at you. It is, however, possible to use this approach to counter those thoughts, as and when they happen. It helps when you label each thought.

VOICE EXERCISE:

Countering your inner voice

Go back to your Stuck workbook and find: stucknowwhat.com/resources

Take two to three minutes to:

1. Write down a thought from your inner voice.

2. Sit with it for a moment.

3. Then counter it by coming up with your own truth.

As you do this more and you become confident, you will start to have some fun with your inner voice.

Step 2: Create your own personal board, similar to that of an executive board committee in an organisation

Let's look at the second part of utilising and amplifying your voice. This focuses on how you create your own personal board, and skipping or neglecting this part will result in you relying only on your own voice. After all, when you only have one voice, you have a limited perspective. You're unlikely to see something that someone with a different perspective can see clearly, e.g. you might see your best route to being promoted as one thing but your mentor/manager (or even coach) might see it as something else.

Organisational and committee boards tend to have different personalities around the table. Within the board environment, there will exist challenge and discussion as well as agreement and consensus. Their functions and roles are to navigate and steer the business towards achieving its own vision and vision of success. This is often broken down into business strategies, which in turn filter down to objectives.

What is a personal board?

A personal board is a group made up of people who you trust, respect and can seek advice from. They provide a different perspective for you and may challenge you better than you would yourself and they may also have connections in their network that you don't. Whilst you're not looking to bring people together as such, you are looking to give some thought and consideration to who you can have on your personal board. Think of them as a wise counsel of advisors. One you can seek guidance from, with each person bringing their own skills/experience to the table.

Having a personal board will add to your voice; in fact, to be able to have different conversations with specific people will be hugely empowering and encouraging. Choosing the people who can provide a mixture of advice, challenges, encouragement and authority is key to having a successful personal board.

A simple way of choosing who you have on your personal board can be by using the work of Carl Jung on archetypes. This is a concept that I've used over and over again with individuals who are stuck in their current role and business owners (entrepreneurs) wanting to grow their business. It's effective and can help move you forward quicker than if you'd just relied on yourself.

Archetypes are people with certain characteristics who behave in different ways. We are going to look at four key archetypes. These are the types of people that you should be looking to include on your personal board.

They are referred to as:

- King/Queen

- Friend/Lover

- Warrior/Challenger

- Magician/Teacher

Each archetype, and therefore person, on your board will offer you something different. Naturally, each of us will default to one or two of these archetypes in our own lives. Think about how you tend to show up each day and how you interact with others. As you read through the descriptions of each, you should recognise certain characteristics and behaviours that you display each day in your work. This will help you in turn to notice the archetypes that are missing in your life right now.

For myself, I tend to default to the warrior/challenger and friend/lover mostly. However, I also provide elements of magician/teacher in the work that I do with individuals and organisations.

What's missing for me is the king/queen. Having this self-awareness first and foremost is key as I will now actively seek others to provide elements of king/queen behaviours to fill this gap on my personal board. I will also, though, seek other support, wisdom and challenge from the other archetypes to complement my thinking and empower me even more.

Once you're clear on which archetypes you default to, then ask yourself: who do you need to add to your personal board? You want all four archetypes to be present in order to support you in your quest to achieve your vision of success. It's worth noting here that you are not limited to one of each archetype and you can have as many people on your board as you desire.

Here's a description of each archetype:

King/Queen:

- Someone who provides some authority.

- Someone who we look to for approval.

- We turn to them for advice.

- We look up to them.

- We want boundaries from them.

- We respect them and take their advice.

- They don't often speak to us.

- Like a good boss or mentor, they want to draw self-leadership out of us.

- They're not going to do a lot of directing and this can be frustrating.

- They will keep you on track and you will seek their approval.

- They command respect because they've walked the ground before you, usually.

- Or they may have led us (in the past) in a way that we admire.

- In their absence we feel purposeless.

Friend/Lover:

- Tends to be the more intimate figure(s) in our lives.

- They could be a sibling or best friend or partner.

- We can unashamedly be ourselves in their company.

- We value them for who they are and so they can just be themselves.

- They speak from the heart.

- They bring us relaxation.

- They talk about the positives that we bring to life.

- They come from a place of 'just be yourself'.

- There's no pressure from them for us to improve.

- We feel lonely when they are absent.

- We become over focused and serious when they're missing.

- When they're missing from our lives, people may experience us as being insensitive.

Warrior/Challenger:

- They play a sharpening role in our life.

- They are the one who points the finger at us and calls us out.

- They stand for our improvement.

- The warrior will face us down.

- They'll point out our rackets and challenge our laziness.

- If we collapse or fall, they will stand us back up again.

- They make us face conversations that we don't want to have.

- They are for us and challenge us to be the best version of ourselves.

- They encourage us to be honest with ourselves, to be brave and face into our challenges.

- Fear doesn't worry them, it drives them.

- When they are not present, we make allowances for ourselves and let distractions in.

Magician/Teacher:

- Previously, they were known and seen as nomads.

- They are great at providing a reframe or offering some sound advice.

- They get us to consider another perspective.

- They often provide or suggest a different form of thinking.

- Through metaphors they offer alternative learning from a situation.

- They will give us new insights.

- They'll also highlight unseen truths.

- When they're not present, we can become insular.

- Without them, our potential becomes capped and our circle narrows.

VOICE EXERCISE:

Putting your personal board together

Assembling your personal board should be fun and enjoyable. If you have explored this process before then feel free to jump ahead to the example below.

1. Start by asking yourself: Who do you know that has certain characteristics of each of the archetypes that you would like to have on your personal board? They can be in your current place of work or outside of work. They don't have to include your current manager, though in some cases your manager may be already providing you with something based on their default archetype(s).

2. Fill out a list in the worksheet in your Stuck workbook.

3. On this list, who can fulfil the archetype roles that are missing in terms of what you naturally default to yourself?

4. On this list, who can complement and add to the archetype roles that you naturally default to yourself?

5. Now you've started to create your personal board, it's time to get clear on what it is you're looking for from each board member.

Example: The Sales Manager (in Chapter 7)

A short reminder: This Sales Manager was bold enough, and open enough, to be vulnerable in front of his peers. He had a clear vision of success, being Sales Director within two years, and is progressing on that journey.

When he's in work, he defaults to the Warrior/Challenger archetype.

Archetypes on his personal board – currently:

King/Queen:

In typical Salesperson fashion, my King is my Sales Director as he is my boss, my mentor and my yardstick for success. Tangibly, he controls my money and my development, but emotionally, he dictates my confidence, my pride and my drive.

The relationship is a myriad of subtle signals. The trust manifests itself in his distance, the respect is communicated by his straight-talking, and the confidence is evident through the scarcity of his acclaim or celebration; it's what he expects now. It is the boundaries that make that rare pat-on-the-back all the sweeter. My King provides advice, guidance and that light, mostly light, nudge that is required when I start to stumble from the path.

Magician/Teacher:

For a long time, I thought of myself as the Teacher because I knew, or believed I knew, the answers to everything within my realm. It was only when I considered 'How can I be teaching anyone anything if I am being asked the same questions every day?' that I allowed myself to be taught, and the Teacher who has led me to this realisation is Jeff. My experience of, and continued relationship with, Jeff allows me to achieve a lot more through asking rather than telling.

I solve problems now by allowing the owner of the problem to reverse-engineer the situation and, ultimately, identify the true problem themselves. I ask 'Why?' before saying 'You should.' However, the real 'magic' of this archetype is the insight. An alternative viewpoint from Jeff, or at least a scenario being positioned differently, facilitates a more democratic and empathetic approach to my problem solving.

Archetypes missing from his personal board – currently:

Friend/Lover:

Although I have these relationships in my life, I still find it difficult to show any vulnerability when discussing work-related issues or stresses. It is not a judgement on the Friend/Lover characters in my life, or a lack of trust; it is more to do with me. I believe that the stresses of the role simply come with the territory and it's what I'm paid to handle; so, by that principle, I don't believe in putting that burden on anyone else, especially someone who I would class as a

Friend or Lover. The distinction between opening up and complaining is something that I have always struggled with.

My takeaway from this is to explore my existing relationships inside of work and be open to those people contributing to my personal board in the Friend/Lover role. There are people in my life that I'm comfortable to be myself around; I just need to put aside the 'head of sales' part of myself and let them see me.

Warrior/Challenger:

My Warrior/Challenger is not embodied. I have my own drivers and my resolve is fairly well calloused at this point in my career but, in terms of my personal board, there is not a particular individual fulfilling the Warrior/Challenger role.

There are elements of the Warrior/Challenger archetype in my King and my Teacher, in that they challenge me, they call me out and, most importantly, they pick me up when I fall. As far as having one person who keeps me sharp through constant challenging, that seat on my board is empty.

If I were to be kind, or ignorant, then I could tell myself that I am simply so self-motivated that the Warrior/Challenger role is redundant on my personal board. If I were to be humble, or honest, then it is more likely that my reaction to being challenged in the past has made the Challenger role on my board quite difficult to recruit for.

To summarise, in relation to the example above, the Sales Director is now looking at his personal board in a couple of ways.

Firstly, he's looking at who he has in his network that can provide 'support' (Friend/Lover) and 'sharpening' (Warrior/Challenger). Secondly, whilst he may continue to seek 'authority' from his King and 'wisdom' from his Teacher, there is always value in being open to having others provide characteristics from these archetypes in the future.

For you, your personal board is something that you control, and it will make a difference to what you're doing right now. Being aware of the people around you and utilising them in the form of your personal board, will help you to evolve and continue to grow. As you reconnect with people in your network and start developing relationships with new people outside of your current network, they too can help you to amplify your voice.

We began this chapter by looking at your own voice and your confidence to share your ideas with others. We all know someone in our lives who's said that it's too late for them, or that the opportunity has passed them by. Perhaps you may have said this yourself?! Well, I'd like to share a story that challenges that thought and shows the power of the voice when we are prepared to share our ideas.

The Olympic rower who had the courage to commit

Back in 2019 I was fortunate to spend some time interviewing Greg Searle for my podcast. Having previously had Kriss Akabusi MBE (and winner of countless medals of all colours!) and Kate Richardson-Walsh OBE (Olympic gold and bronze medallist) on the show, I was excited to understand more about Greg's journey.

To give you a little bit of background, Greg won Olympic gold (with his brother) in rowing at the Barcelona games in 1992, at the age of 20. Four years later at the Atlanta games he won a bronze medal. At Sydney in 2000, aged 28 and at his peak in terms of physical fitness, he came fourth.

Greg then moved away from rowing and did some work as a consultant in the learning and development space, whilst also doing some other things, including speaking. Twelve years later, in 2012, he was competing once more, aged 40, at the London Olympic Games.

The full episode of the podcast is available to download and listen to via iTunes or Spotify – just search for *Jeff Weigh*.

About ten minutes into our discussion, I asked him, 'What got you back in the boat?' Essentially, whilst doing some other things, he'd got to learn from other people, people who had had different experiences to him. He'd stayed fit and healthy and continued rowing a couple of times each week.

When the London 2012 bid to host the games was announced, it was with the strapline of 'Inspire a Generation'. The process concluded with London being successful in their bid, as we all know. Once the Olympic dates for each event had been announced, Greg quickly realised that the rowing final would be on 2nd August 2012. That was exactly 20 years on from when he'd won his gold medal, on 2nd August 1992.

His inner voice started to dream, imagining what it would be like to repeat his achievement of 20 years earlier and play a part in inspiring a generation. His children would be 9 and 11 at the time of the final.

Two events subsequently happened in late 2008 and in 2009 that helped his mind switch. Firstly, he'd broken his leg whilst playing five-a-side football, so he would spend the start of 2009 on crutches. His motivation, as it turned out, was a prebooked snowboarding holiday with family and friends planned for the February; in order to snowboard, he had to get fit. This allowed him to get back into the habit of training.

The second event, later in 2009, was the Rowing World Championships. Greg was commentating at this event in Poland. The day after the championships had finished, his flight home was delayed. As he sat in the airport, the rest of the rowing world literally passed him by. He couldn't get home, so – in his words – he hit the pause button. In those 24 hours of being delayed, he made a decision; he was going to come back and compete.

What happened next?

Three years out of competing is a long time in sport, so he clearly had a lot of work to do. Driving to Nottingham (after being delayed coming back to the UK) to work with a client, he rang his wife and told her about his thoughts. He got emotional, as did his wife; she'd been there throughout. This was something they could achieve together, and it would become an adventure that they would share.

The first thing Greg did on arriving home was jump on the rowing machine. He needed to know what he could do and, more importantly, where he was beginning from. Remember, the cold hard facts have no time for excuses! Then it was time to be bold and speak with the head coach about a comeback – although at first he thought Greg was referring to a coaching role.

The head coach set out the performance parameters (as with any other athlete) and then it was down to Greg to do the work and in his words, 'Jump over a lot of hurdles.'

Fast forward to the London Olympic Games in 2012 and Greg was part of the bronze medal winning eight. Whilst they didn't win the gold medal, which was their vision of success, Greg is extremely proud of his achievement and the fact that he was able to compete in a home Games with his family and friends there to witness the occasion.

Greg's story, like those of other successful sporting people, demonstrates the 6 Vs very well. Starting out with a clear vision of success, coupled with strong values, provided the foundation for the journey that was ahead of him. Even though success is never guaranteed in sport, it's hugely important to always be aware of your view and current reality.

The vehicle invariably changes from game to game and having the valour to try different things and keep going is often what makes the differences in the end. In fact, having the courage to speak up and have a voice in any team sport or environment is a necessity. The collective voices are what create togetherness and separate the good from the great.

Personal reflection

For me, this is the most important of all the 6 Vs. In part, it is because I have never lost sight of that seven-year-old boy in front of his classmates. I struggled to find my voice, and this was often reinforced as I was being labelled the quiet one in the family. I suppose I was and still am, if you were to line me up alongside my brother.

It's not just for personal reasons that I see this as being such an important stage in the process. I've observed others through my coaching practice who have neglected or not given this stage the focus it requires or deserves. They take it all on themselves and, on those occasions, everything has been just that little bit harder.

The voice stage of the process is so important in supporting and enabling you to achieve your vision of success. It can be easy to overlook it or start to think that you've got it, but you shouldn't. I know I didn't value it enough in the early days. For me, finding my voice and speaking up and out at the start didn't come naturally; sharing my dreams and asking for help was totally alien to me. However, this is something I have worked on and continue to maximise every day.

Here's the crazy thing. The moment I sought the help of others and opened up, I found they were only too ready to listen. Doors started to open and conversation after conversation followed. Many of the people I didn't think I could get close to and learn from all of a sudden made time for me. They were interested and curious to hear what I wanted to do, especially those who had walked a similar path before me; they acted as mentors and provided the wisdom of their experiences.

We each have been given a voice. In most instances, we haven't been shown how to use it to its maximum. This is in no way about having an ego or being an arse; and it's not about flooding different social media channels with just noise either. It's about learning how to put your voice to good use.

Many of the greats who have walked the earth before us have learned to master their voice and harness it for good effect. Every single one of those greats, at different times in their lives, will have called upon others to provide them with a mix of advice, challenge, encouragement and authority.

You and I are no different. Your voice is ready to be heard, so take this opportunity in front of you and embrace the challenges ahead. As the Stoics would say, accept each day, good, bad or otherwise. Work through your plan and commit to daily acts of valour. But know that you are not alone, so call out to those people who can help. Discover for yourself, as I have, that there are some brilliant human beings on this little planet of ours called Earth. The time for your voice is now.

— Key takeaways ━━━━━━━━━━━━━━━

- Learn to sit with your thoughts and challenge your inner voice with some of your own truths.

- Know that you don't have to do it all on your own; very few people do... if ever!

- Start building your own personal board today and surround yourself with the key archetypes.

- Keep going and don't let your hard work (so far) go to waste.

— Questions to consider ━━━━━━━━━

1. What are some of the positive thoughts of your inner voice that you can also use to counter the negative ones?

2. What has got you this far on your journey? (Remind yourself and keep going.)

3. Who would be your 'dream person' to add to your personal board (someone you admire and respect)?

4. What do you want from them and when can you approach them for their advice, challenge, encouragement or authority?

5. As you achieve the next step(s), how will you feel? (Celebrate the small wins, because you deserve to.)

CHAPTER 13

TAKING ACTION

'A journey of a thousand miles begins with a single step.'

LAO TZU

What next?

I've never been a fan of endings and much prefer beginnings. Yes, you've almost reached the end of the book, yet for many of you, your journey is just beginning.

My one hope when I set out to write this book was that, by the end of it, you'd be armed with strategies that you can apply to your working life straight away. Alongside these strategies, you'll also have the confidence to act and, for some, seek the support of a coach who'll keep you accountable and on track.

Now, perhaps more than ever before, you have clarity over where you are in your life and exactly where you want to be in the future. The opportunity to do more work that is aligned with your personal values is hugely empowering and, for some of you, it will be life-changing. These two things alone, when an organisation is supportive, will transform the work that you do and the impact that you can have in a business.

We now live and exist (in some cases) in a world that doesn't sleep, where it has become increasingly harder to switch off. The daily grind is real; you've felt it and been part of it. The striving for the next thing and the next thing can be ever so tempting. By merely stopping and pausing for a moment, you have given yourself the space to take stock and reflect on many aspects of your life right now.

Success is often disguised as hard work, yet the hard work ahead can also be fun work. By crafting a plan that excites you, it means that you're in the driving seat this time. Perhaps that's scary, but it can be equally empowering as well. Safe in the knowledge that, alongside you, you're able to call on others to provide wisdom, support and encouragement along the way.

Take a deep breath, followed by your first step.

The daily grind is real;
you've felt it and been
part of it.

Coaching tips – momentum builders

I've put together some things that I've found really helpful for my clients when it comes to keeping that momentum going.

1. Journaling

Track your progress through writing in a journal daily; it's amazing how quickly writing things down sharpens your mind and focuses you each day. Just 15 minutes in the morning and 15 minutes in the evening is all you need to commit. If you aren't able to commit 30 minutes a day, then start with something smaller like 5 minutes and build up from there. It's such a great way of capturing progress and looking ahead. I promise that you won't regret it.

You can order a journal from the 'Stuck now what' website that's been designed specially to be used alongside the 6 Vs model. If journaling is new to you, don't panic; I've created a guide that will show you how you can get started and make this part of each day. Download the 'How to maximise your journaling' pdf on the 'Stuck now what' website to support you in achieving your vision of success.

2. Commit to one action each day

Whenever I'm working one-on-one with a client, I'll always encourage them to share with me what their first step is. I can hear myself saying out loud, 'What <u>one</u> thing can you do today?' I'm not wanting the list of everything they're planning to do, and I won't accept it when someone responds with, 'By the end of the week I'll do x.'

I'm looking for two things; commitment and intention. The intention of 'I will.' And the commitment of 'By the end of today.' You know yourself that there's a big difference between 'I can' and 'I will'.

Momentum comes from the Latin word '*movere*', which means to move. By seeking commitment and sensing intention, I'm not allowing the person in front me what I call 'wriggle room'. By making that commitment and following through with your intention, you take the first step because you are saying 'I will.' Once you have taken that first step, then you have momentum. You've begun and you're off.

3. Energy management

There will be days when you just want to do a bit more, and that's OK. Before you do, though, just check in with yourself and gauge where your energy levels are. Your plan might state: spend an hour or so completing task 'x'. If you've got no energy left at the end of your day, then an hour or so can turn into two or three hours and you may still have not completed task 'x'.

In those situations, you're better off not trying to complete task 'x' that day. Look back at the day and notice the moments and people who have either given you energy or drained your energy. Try to limit (or remove if possible) the people and moments that drain your energy. You may have put off task 'x' for now, but only until you have the necessary energy to complete it.

Managing your energy is so important during this process. Be kind to yourself in these moments.

4. Balance

One of the challenges that you (and many others) face will be your own balance. The old model of work–life balance isn't particularly helpful and may only hinder you on your journey. The pressure of trying to achieve balance whilst having a burst of energy to get started with something is unrealistic. Take it from someone who spent three years trying to find a better work–life balance. I've given up searching!

Typically, when you find yourself out of balance, it's because you're working towards achieving a goal, objective or your vision of success. Fact. It's part of the process.

What can help you and serve you well is something called a 'perfect imbalance'. A perfect imbalance is where you're aware of when you're going to be out of balance. You consciously choose to take yourself out of balance for a specific purpose and fixed amount of time.

For example, be honest with yourself that for the next couple of weeks while you are trying to achieve a certain goal, you won't be available as much for your family or socialising at the weekends.

You've prepared for it and shared it with those people closest to you. In fact, they should know, because you've been including them in your personal board and sharing with them your vision of success.

However, you need to be aware of when you have become too imbalanced, when your energy starts to flag and you need to take a break – it could be just half an hour or it could be a number of days. You will know what's right and when you feel ready to tackle your tasks. Build in moments of downtime that will allow for some recharging as this will ensure that your balance is in a healthy place.

A perfect imbalance can be an empowering alternative to striving for a work–life balance. You can find out how others take care of their balance by listening to episodes on the Jeff Weigh podcast.

But what if...?

What if you start down this journey towards your vision of success and then something happens? What do you do then? Well, let's be honest, stuff is going to happen to all of us when we start to bring about change. I see this with every client I coach, and I find myself reminding them that it's natural and normal.

Knowing where you are at any point in time is what's really important. Having worked through the 6 Vs, you'll still get stuck or be unsure what to do at times. You always have the option to go back and read over each of the 6 Vs. Alternatively, you can sign up to the 6 Steps to Achieving Your Vision of Success programme on www.stucknowwhat.com. In addition to that, here are some shortcuts to help you:

1. What if... your Vision starts to fade?

It's easy to get caught up with what you're doing. I call this being in the now. You're only focused on today and getting through it. Nothing else gets a look in. You're not even thinking about the future. The road ahead becomes foggy or hazy.

In this situation:

- Revisit your vision of success.

- Remind yourself why it's important to you.

- Think about how you'll feel, what you'll see and what you'll hear others say when you achieve your vision of success.

- If your vision of success seems too far away, create a shorter-term vision of success as well. Something that's closer, a milestone if you like, which will feel more achievable.

This will remove some of the fog or the haze and bring clarity back to you. In turn, this will empower you to maintain that focus.

2. What if... your Values start to get over-whelmed?

As you know from earlier chapters, you will face obstacles on your journey. One of the biggest tensions can be if you're working outside of your personal values. This means that you're doing things that don't sit with your values.

It's normal for this to happen. In organisations especially, you can spend a lot of time doing work outside of your values.

In this situation:

- Firstly, notice when this happens. It's usually when something feels like more of an effort to you. Or when you're hesitating with a particular task.

- If it's happening a lot, be bold and have a conversation with your manager about it.

- Also, pause for a moment and look at the work you're actually doing. Ask yourself, 'What can I change within my work that will allow me to work more within my values?'

- It may mean delegating certain tasks or handing over responsibility to others. Many of these things will within your control.

Don't sit and suffer when there's actions to be taken; you'll thank yourself afterwards for acting. When you are working within your personal values, it feels more natural and you get into a flow state.

3. What if... your View starts to shift?

Here's the thing about your view: it's always shifting. Take a few steps towards your vision of success and pause for a moment. Look back and you're no longer where you were, or where you started.

Avoid the downfall that is often associated with various diets. You lose a few pounds, look back at where you were, and start to feel good about yourself. A takeaway here and a glass of wine there and you're back where you started. I always smile when people say to me: 'I'm going back to Slimming World because that worked for me.' In many cases, the vision of success wasn't clear enough from the outset.

In this situation:

- Go back and look at your reason for starting (your vision of success).

- It's so important for you to remind yourself at regular points how far you've come, especially if you feel your motivation dipping.

- Check in with your manager or coach.

- Speak to those people around you on your personal board.

- Share your progress and bumps in the road with them.

- Know that the next small action will change your view.

4. What if... your Vehicle starts to get bogged down?

Similar to your view, your vehicle will continue to change and evolve along the way. Remember that you've created your own plan and you can change that plan. Some tasks will take more time and thought than others.

If you find yourself procrastinating, then simply do the next task. Make that your intention and give it your full attention until it's completed. This way you'll avoid the many distractions that will invariably appear.

In this situation:

- Capture your progress in your journal.

- Regularly revisit the Daily–Weekend and Priority Trackers to understand where your time and energy are going.

As my good friend, Ian Braid says, 'You can't fill from an empty jug.' Give yourself permission to take 'minibreaks' from the plan. If need be, plan them in.

- Fill your jug and then go again.

5. What if... your Valour starts to waver?

Once you make your first bold, brave decision, then you're on your way. As I've just shared, your view changes and you'll quickly find yourself moving through the tasks that were part of your plan. Because you've created your personal board, you can always draw on those people for advice and support. The reality is that they will have been brave at times in their career and may have trodden a similar path as they moved towards their own vision of success.

I wouldn't have spoken to some amazing people on my podcast over the last two years if I hadn't been brave and just gone for it. Each time I would start with, 'What's the worst that can happen?' The answer being that they would just say no!

The majority, however, say yes. Valour is like compound interest; the more you are courageous, the bigger the payback. Keep reminding yourself: 'Act boldly, time is limited.'

(Courtesy of Jim Lawless – *Taming Tigers*).

In this situation:

- Act boldly, be brave and go for it.

6. What if... your Voice is struck by self-doubt?

As you set off down the path towards achieving your vision of success, your own voice will begin to change. Sure, you'll have days when the negative or unsure inner voice shows up, but over time you'll learn to quieten it down. And, as that voice quietens, your own voice will start to get louder.

It's such a liberating process to experience, especially if you have been quiet for too long. Sadly, many of us have been conditioned to fit into the social norm or family and generational expectations. I believe we have been designed to stand out, rather than to fit in.

The great thing is that when you start to find your voice and to stand out, you realise that you're not alone.

'Don't let what you cannot do interfere with what you can do.'

EMPOWERING WORDS FROM JOHN R WOODEN

The people who you've selected to be on your personal board will become some of your greatest champions. When you've surrounded yourself with people who want you to do well, anything feels possible.

In this situation:

- Use your personal board, it can be your friend when you need it most.

FINAL THOUGHTS

'What day is it?' asked Pooh.

'It's today,' squeaked Piglet.

'My favourite day,' said Pooh.

A A MILNE

This has been one of my favourite quotes for some time and we have this hanging on the wall in our study at home. What I love about it is that every day it provides me with an opportunity to make a choice. I'm genuinely one of those 'half-full glass' type of people. When I read this quote, it inspires and empowers me; even when things aren't going well, it reminds me I can still do something today. It gives me the chance to reframe things; however small, a little movement in the right direction is enough.

Every time I sat down to write a part of this book, this quote was at the forefront of my mind. Five hundred words or an hour later and I was happy; I'd tell myself that I'd done what I needed to do that day. When I wrote more or did some further research, they were both a bonus. As I passed a thousand words, or completed a chapter, I smiled and then repeated my efforts the following day. I never lost sight of the end goal and, with each chapter written, my confidence and belief simply grew stronger.

If an hour a day is too much for you right now, then start smaller. One percent of your day is 14.4 minutes – let's call it 15. Commit yourself to spending one percent of your day working towards your vision of success and watch what happens in one, three, six, twelve months and so on.

Stop 'Losing your Sunday to your Monday' as Gavin Oattes says on the Jeff Weigh podcast.

Start taking action today, and know that there's support there should you need it, whether that's through your own personal board or by working with a coach. Discover more at *Stucknowwhat.com* and join the Facebook community and connect with similar people who have taken control of their lives and are working towards achieving their own vision of success. It's a fun community and another vehicle to support you along your journey.

Feel empowered and no longer stuck.

Find joy and satisfaction in your work.

Make the changes needed to your work situation.

You can do this, and you deserve this.

Big love, Jeff

WHAT NEXT?

Firstly, congratulations on making your way through this book. Millions of people in the world find themselves stuck but very few grab that bull by the horns and do something about it.

You are now well on your way towards the fulfilling career you deserve. This book is the beginning of that journey. You need to put the 6Vs into action and I've got a whole host of ways to help you do that on a website that we created specifically for readers of the book wanting to take their careers to the next level:

http://www.stucknowwhat.com

The natural next steps for you would be to join me on either of the following:

- 6 Steps to Achieving your Vision of Success. A one-day programme where you deep-dive into the 6Vs and create your own road map to facilitate your journey to success. This is the quickest and most impactful way for you to reignite your career.

- 'Live' Learning sessions. These are monthly bite-sized learning sessions (45 minutes long) where you can join others to learn, share and support one another.

On the website you'll also be able to get your hands on the book resources (these will be invaluable to you if you are yet to do the exercises in the book):

- 1 Page Overview. A printable overview of the 6V Framework which you can keep in your journal or put up near your desk.

- The Stuck! Now what? Workbook. A downloadable workbook containing all of the exercises in the book, allowing you to make notes and work through each section without writing all over your book.

Consistency is the key for any transformation, and consistent reminders and digestion of information relating to it keeps your goal at the forefront of your mind. Which is exactly why I created my podcast where you'll find regular little nuggets of insight, inspiration and interviews with interesting individuals from the world of sport, business and academia.

Search for 'Jeff Weigh' on Spotify or Apple Podcasts

A QUICK FAVOUR

If you've got this far in the book I sincerely hope you've enjoyed what you've read. To spread the word and help others out there, like you, who are stuck, it would really mean a lot to me if you could hop back over to Amazon and leave a review of the book so that other potential readers can see what you got out of it.

Connect with me

I'm always keen to connect with and hear from my readers for any feedback, things you are struggling with or what you've found helpful. Please come and say hello on social media. You can find me at:

WWW.LINKEDIN.COM/IN/JEFFWEIGH/

TWITTER.COM/JEFF_WEIGH

WWW.INSTAGRAM.COM/JEFFWEIGH/

RECOMMENDED READING

Atomic Habits: An easy and proven way to build good habits and break bad ones
James Clear

Dying for a Paycheck: How modern management harms employee health and company performance and what we can do about it
Jeffrey Pfeffer

Ego is the Enemy: The fight to master our greatest opponent
Ryan Holiday

Essentialism: The disciplined pursuit of less
Greg McKeown

How to Get Control of Your Time and Your Life
Alan Lakein

Meditations – Marcus Aurelius: A new translation
Gregory Hays

Taming Tigers: Do things you never thought you could
Jim Lawless

The Chimp Paradox: The mind management programme for confidence, success and happiness
Dr Steve Peters

The Magic of Work: How you can balance your soul work and salary work
Mike Pegg

The Obstacle is the Way: The ancient art of turning adversity to advantage
Ryan Holiday

The Subtle Art of Not Giving a Fuck: A counterintuitive approach to living a good life
Mark Manson

Tools of Titans: The tactics, routines and habits of billionaires, icons and world-class performers
Tim Ferriss

ACKNOWLEDGEMENTS

With so many people to thank, it's difficult to know where to start.

I have been blessed to have had an enormous amount of support and encouragement over the last 10 years so I apologise if I've not referred to you in this part of the book.

Firstly, I'd like to thank my wife, Emma, the most supportive person in my life. Secondly, I'd like to thank the team at Known Publishing for making this young boy's dream a reality. Even before I walked into your office in March 2020, you got my passion and understood what I was looking to do. The first day of lockdown will be fixed in my memory for the rest of my life. Thank you to Leila for your challenge, patience, support and encouragement; you've made me a better writer as a result of your time and persistence. Thank you to Ali for your energy, belief, knowledge and ideas; you've pushed me outside of my comfort zone continuously. You've both been such a key part in enabling me to find the words to share my voice. Thank you to the support team at Known Publishing as well, who have read and re-read the manuscript many times and provided sound feedback on every single occasion.

Thank you to my personal support team, or the 'band' as I often refer to them. I've felt like Columbo at times asking of you 'just one more thing.' To James Farrell, Scott Leiper, Kirsty Mac, Olga Piehler, Emma Davis, Richmond Stace, Declan O'Connell, Mark, Elliott, Emma Dechoux, Di Murray, Chris Lovett and Ben Hardman. Your feedback on the 6 V chapters in particular and input into the subsequent programmes has been invaluable. I hope we'll come together and share many more gigs!

I'd like to extend my thanks to several other people who I've met along this journey and who I've shared my crazy ideas with. Jim McNeish, Osmaan Sharif, Chris Barez-Brown, Phil White, Garry Turner, Ian Braid, Meg Moore, Tim Roberts, Kieran McCourt, Kevin McAlpin, Michel Falcon, Greg Searle, Simon Austin and Cody Royle. You've all challenged my thinking in many ways and helped me become a better version of myself. You've also become friends for life, and I'm truly thankful for that.

Thank you to the guides, sages and mentors. Here are a few to note. Dig Woodvine who taught me the importance of family and, in particular, time with family. Miles Hilton-Barber who inspired me and provoked me to dream bigger! Kirsty Mac who was the catalyst to all of this and who helped me to start to believe in myself. It's definitely a lifetime association now! Jim Lawless who inspired me long before I met him, through his book Taming Tigers and rule number 1; act boldly, time is limited. His words – 'we are writing the story of our lives' – act as a constant reminder to keep going each day and make the most of our time. Kriss Akabusi, one of my heroes as a kid growing up watching athletics. Our conversations on philosophy and life encouraged me to continue to explore and learn. Mike Pegg, your generosity in terms of time and wisdom (especially during lockdown 1.0) has been well received and put to good use. Having a clear picture of success is in my consciousness because of you and a key ingredient in lives of many people including myself.

Thank you to all the organisations and individual clients that I have had the pleasure to work with and serve over the last 10 years. There's so many I could mention and some that I can't (due to NDAs). It really has been a joy and you've helped me to learn along the way.

At times we need others to give us a chance and I'm grateful to the leaders at Dovenest, Performance Coaching International, VA Consultants and Raise the Bar for doing just that. Giving me the opportunity to be part of your teams has helped me to grow. Thank you.

My family have always been and continue to be there for me, supporting me with my many crazy ideas. Mum has always bestowed the importance of being happy and has been there when things haven't gone to plan. My first wife Jo (and her family) supported me when I made my first leap of faith in leaving M&S Money in 2010 and I'll always be grateful to them.

My brothers, Dan and Steve, both provide me with the challenge to make something of myself and I thank them for that. Thank you to the Foden clan for accepting me into your world. We don't come together often enough.

Thank you to Emma, my wife, for her love and support throughout this whole journey and being by my side, nudging me along. At times, she believes in me more than I believe in myself. Her patience in reading through the many drafts and listening to me talk about the book (for what seemed like an eternity) has been unwavering. My biggest fan, I did it.

I'd like to thank my kids: Becky, Alex and Jess for loving me for who I am and sharing so many special moments. You inspire me each day to be a better person and to think about my contribution to the world. When you find yourself stuck, know that I'm here to help you to find the answers that you need.

Last but by no means least, thank you to each of my dads. My dad and my father-in-law, both called David; you both left this world way too soon and I wish I could share a beer or two with you both. My other dad, Kenny, a wise man with a big heart; you taught me the importance of listening and selective hearing. I endeavour each day to get this right.

ENDNOTES

1 https://www.independent.co.uk/life-style/average-commute-time-59-min-utes-record-work-tuc-a9204031.htm

2 https://www.businessleader.co.uk/how-many-days-of-work-are-lost-from-snoozing-an-alarm/54602/

3 https://www.theguardian.com/commentisfree/2016/feb/01/loneli-ness-at-work-introvert-sadness-bereft-in-bustling-office

4 https://www.inc.com/adam-robinson/new-study-finds-40-percent-of-em-ployees-feel-isolated-heres-how-to-make-your-workplace-more-inclusive-and-productive.html

5 https://www.inc.com/adam-robinson/new-study-finds-40-percent-of-em-ployees-feel-isolated-heres-how-to-make-your-workplace-more-inclusive-and-productive.html

6 https://www.hse.gov.uk/stress/

7 British Pain Society, 2016

8 Societal Impact of Pain, 2017

9 https://people-first.com/blog/?page=8

10 https://www.bbc.com/worklife/article/20190610-how-to-tell-if-youve-got-pre-burnout

11 https://jamesclear.com/new-habit

12 https://jamesclear.com/new-habit

Lightning Source UK Ltd.
Milton Keynes UK
UKHW011841210921
390971UK00001B/35